The CHURCH

is Supposed
to be

DIFFEЯENT

Denise L. Shaw

Denise L. Shaw
1 Cor 3:18

The Church is Supposed to be Different
978-0-9891429-9-1
Copyright © 2019 by Denise L. Shaw

Published by Mountz Media & Publishing
Tulsa, OK 74137
www.mountzmedia.com

Endorsements

I have known Denise Shaw for many years and observed her dedication in the service of the Lord. Her readers will find much food to chew on in considering the amazing authoritative position of the body of Christ.

Dr. Billye Brim
Branson, Missouri

As I read the book written by Denise Shaw, *The Church Is Supposed to be Different*, I have been blessed, encouraged, and motivated by her wonderful stories, testimonies, and Bible teaching woven all together to form a very powerful message and gift to the body of Christ. This book is a matrix of solid biblical truths that will affirm many in their calling and challenge all who read it to dig deeper into their relationship with Christ.

Keith E. Taylor
Lead Pastor Cross Tabernacle Church
Founder Gilgal Ministries
Terre Haute, Indiana

A book designed for the WHOLE body of Christ. By precept and example, the text cuts through denominational barriers and lays to rest doctrinal differences. Written in a succinct and compelling manner, it brings reality to the profound truths of who we, the body of Christ, are and what our destiny is in Him.

Rev. Cathy Creek
Creek Ministries, Inc.
Broken Arrow, Oklahoma

The Church Is Supposed to be Different is a statement that we all can agree on. However, few are those who know how it should be different or how to get there! Denise Shaw goes into detail of how it should be different and how to get there by sharing her heart and what she has learned over the years of ministry. She makes a statement toward the beginning of this book that echoes what I've been saying about my generation: "We are entering a time now when we must tell what we know to help one another understand spiritual realities that are often overlooked or misunderstood."

Steadfastly gaze upon the vision, the plan, and the purpose. Never lose sight of our destiny! This quote by Denise pretty much describes what she has labored with much prayer and love to instill in this book! I have gleaned so much from the chapters in this book that each chapter is my favorite chapter! I highly recommend this book to you and encourage you to read each chapter prayerfully as it will reveal to you what God is looking for in His Church and what the Church will be like when He returns!

Prophet Fred Aguilar
Indianapolis, Indiana

Denise Shaw has written a great book that calls the church back to her roots. This book is soundly written, and it will inspire you to be different as God intended for you to be.

Pastor Randall Burton
Northview Assembly of God
Columbus, Indiana

CONTENTS

To Bryan

My constant companion, the prophet of our home.
It brings me great joy to share this journey with you.

In Loving Memory

Dean Neihart Kelley
September 21, 1936 ~ September 26, 1997
My biggest fan.

His Hands Tell the Story

Daddy was a simple man who worked hard all his life,
He tilled the soil and planted every season with his wife,
Anxiously waiting to see the crops grow every year,
His passion was the harvest; it made all sorrow disappear.

Daddy was a craftsman; he loved to work with wood,
He provided for his family every way that he could,
A carpenter by trade and a teacher to me,
He was a fine example of what my life's supposed to be.

And at the end of his life his hands would tell the story,
Many sacrifices made, the scars were plain to see,
He extended his hands for the benefit of others,
Oh, how great the price he paid to meet my need.

Jesus was no ordinary man, of God He was a part,
He sowed the Word and planted in the soil of men's hearts,
He touched the multitudes for just a few short years,
His passion was the harvest; to make all sorrow disappear.

Jesus was a man of sorrows, touched with the feelings of our fears,
He provided for our needs; He came to dry every tear,
A carpenter by trade; a Teacher to you and me,
He was a fine example of what our life's supposed be.

And at the end of His life His hands would tell the story,
The final sacrifice was made; His scars were plain to see,
He extended His hands for the salvation of others,
Oh, how great the price He paid so that all men could be free!

FOREWORD

Why should you read this book?

Most of us are very busy—probably too busy. Because of that we find ourselves becoming more cautious about what we allow to take our time. So, I ask again why should you take time to read this book? Let me suggest four reasons to you.

Firstly, the book is timely. The principles Denise explores and explains are timeless but many of us believe we are living in one of the most significant time frames in history. The coming of the Lord, the end time revival, and the turmoil of contemporary history are coming together. This book will help give understanding not only about the season but specifically what you can be as a part of the "church that is supposed to be different."

Secondly, the book is well written. Some people have things of importance to say but cannot say them well. Others have nothing to say but at least they say that nothing in a way that holds your attention. Denise has been given something to say by the Spirit, and she says it well. That is in itself, "something different."

Thirdly, the book deals with gut level issues from the Bible. Death… sickness…finances…family…joy…job…and much more. Are not these the issues of life? Scripture reveals how to handle these things in a way that is "different," and Denise does a great job of sharing that difference.

Fourthly, the book is not theory. It comes from the life the Lord has given to her and her husband. The stories will resonate. They have power. They will help you. They are helping me.

At the close of the book, Denise talks about returning to Terre Haute, Indiana. I am somewhat aware first-hand of that part of the story. In 2010, my wife and I were invited to preach a three-day meeting at a church in that city. That meeting became much more than any of us would have ever guessed. Denise and Bryan have been used by God in that ongoing move of God and in the many places being impacted by it. I am a witness to that.

I believe as you read this book you will be challenged, perhaps convicted, that your part of the universal church can and will be "different." It is a Glorious Church. Linda and I read the book together over the course of two days. I will read it again. It is ministering to me.

Michael Livengood, International Evangelist
Indiana/New Zealand

INTRODUCTION

"*H*ow long did it take to write the Gettysburg Address?" someone once asked Abraham Lincoln. "My whole life," was his reply. The same could be said about the writing of this book. It has been a lifetime in the making.

In fact, all our lives produce a story a lifetime in the making, and the quality of the story improves with the volume of our lives. We can draw upon the collective experience, allowing God to make something beautiful of it all. After all, it's God who writes the best stories—delivering a hero to save us and a happily ever after for those who believe.

This collection of true-life stories, testimonies, messages, and poems offers real-life examples of how God reaches down His mighty hand and completely transforms the life of a simple believer. May these truths inspire your heart and encourage your soul.

A friend once said, "Denise, you have the most amazing stories. You're kind of like a spiritual 'Forrest Gump.'" I'm certain she intended the comment to be a compliment, but it gave me pause to think. Some of the real-life stories contained herein are what one might term "outlandish," but they are true just the same—every jot and tittle.Some of the accounts shared have been deep spiritual encounters with the Lord—holy moments that are difficult to convey on the written page without discounting their validity or their power. One cannot have encounters such as these without being forever changed and transformed by the power of the living God and His Word.

As the pieces of this work came together *the Church is supposed to be different* was a common theme woven throughout the text. Often, we find the lessons and conclusions drawn speaking of a broader need for change in the body of Christ. Of course, the nature of God is to do a new thing (Isaiah 42:9, Lamentations 3:22-23), which means change is inevitable. And since God does not change (Malachi 3:6), the transformation lies solely with us.

I'm reminded of an old song, *"From glory to glory He's changing me, changing me, changing me. His likeness and image to perfect in me. The love of God shown to the world...."* Believers are all destined to be changed into His likeness and image (2 Corinthians 3:18).

After all, the *Church is supposed to be different!* Different from the way it is now? Different from the rest of the world? Different from the way it has been? Different from what many think it should be? All of the above.

In fact, I pray that *you* will be different as you read the pages that follow. May change come to you as the Father transforms you into all that He's designed you to be so that you may embark on all He's called you to do.

~ Denise Shaw

COURAGEOUS BRIDE REFUSES FEAR

Our Destiny Is to be Glorious

Ephesians 5:26-27

that He [Jesus] might sanctify and cleanse her with the washing of water by the word, that He might present her to Himself a glorious church, not having spot or wrinkle or any such thing, but that she should be holy and without blemish. [brackets mine]

2 Corinthians 6:14 (KJV)

...for what fellowship hath... light with darkness?

In the spring of 1997, the Lord spoke to my heart and said, "Great fear will grip the world in the days to come. If the Church is not careful, that same fear will get over into it." Regardless of current events and news the world over, we're not supposed to be afraid. Believers are to have confidence in our Redeemer, trusting Him for guidance and protection. It may sound like a cliché, but Jesus truly is the answer for the world today. As believers we know The Answer. And it's time for us to act like it.

God's Word makes it clear that there should be a marked difference between believers and the rest of the world. That means we should look different, think different, and act different. We should *be* different.

The Lord also spoke to my heart in 1997 that "in the days ahead, people will run to the glory." The Church is destined to be glorious, bright, and shiny for all the world to see. Christians are supposed to shine as bright as the noonday sun. If we do not, how will they know where to run? Have we taken advantage of every opportunity to win the lost? Could it be that our shininess has been dulled by fear? Could it be that the lost have no desire to turn to the Church for help because many within it are just as scared? Have we lost our luster?

In His Word, God tells us exactly how to shine:

Daniel 11:32
...but the people who know their God shall be strong, and carry out great exploits.

Isaiah 40:29
He gives power to the weak, and to those who have no might He increases strength.

2 Timothy 1:7
For God has not given us a spirit of fear, but of power and of love and of a sound mind.

Now is not the time to cower in the corner like a whimpering pup. Those who know God are to be strong and courageous. God has not given us a spirit of fear, but He's given us power. When we feel like fainting, we should look to Him for the strength to face whatever comes. How can we go to the uttermost parts of the world if we're afraid to get on an airplane? Fear is not of God. It is an evil spirit sent to torment, sent to rob us of our peace of mind and faith. Thank the Lord, we don't have to tolerate an evil attack, and most assuredly, we should never allow ourselves to entertain it. Never be polite to fear! As soon as it shows up, tell it to leave in Jesus' name. It must go!

As a young girl, I learned to entertain fear as I watched my mother pace from window to window at the first sight of a thunderstorm. By the time I was an adolescent, a fear of storms had gripped my life until it was nearly paralyzing. But praise God, when I was a junior in high school, the pastor of our local church taught a series of messages on the authority of the believer, and I learned how to use the name of Jesus. I learned that the evil spirit of fear has to bow to that name. I was intrigued by the thought and eager to give it a try. Within a few weeks, I had the opportunity.

Early one morning, I was awakened by the familiar clap of thunder and bright lightning flashes. My palms began to sweat almost instantly. A suffocating heaviness on my chest made it difficult to breath, and a cold shiver ran down my spine. Fear had become a close personal companion—always there when I needed it the least. It took everything within me to whisper, "Jesus." With resolve, I timidly said, "Fear you have to go in Jesus' name." It left…instantly. Wow! I could breathe!

The enemy is tenacious, but the next time he brought fear to me, it was much easier to command it to go. From then on, I was completely free from fear of bad weather. To this day, I thoroughly enjoy a good thunderstorm as long as it's not destructive. They are a pleasant reminder of the victory found in Jesus that blustery spring morning.

The phrases *fear not* and *be not afraid* appear in the Bible dozens of times. After all, God knew fear would come to us all. That's one of the reasons He gave us His authority and His name. God wants us to deal with fear—not ignore it or hope it goes away. Fear robs us of the very things we hold dear.

Job said, "For the thing which I greatly *feared* is come upon me, and that which I was *afraid* of is come unto me" (Job 3:25 KJV). Some folks like to think that Job's trial came to him because God is mean and unjust, but in examining the previous scripture, we see that fear actually opened the door for destruction. It was God's goodness and mercy that delivered him and restored all that had been lost. What a valuable lesson to be gleaned from Job. You and I can avoid a lot of heartache by refusing to fear.

However, it's important that we don't take this lesson to the extreme. I remember several years ago, after the birth of my first baby, I was suddenly faced with a whole new set of fears—worries that often accompany motherhood. It was a challenge to rise above these fearful thoughts, and in the process, something strange happened. I became afraid to be afraid. I had learned Job's lesson so well that I was afraid to even have a fearful thought.

The enemy tried to bring terrible thoughts to my mind about the safety of my child. As that familiar presence of fear tried to attach itself to me, it was compounded with thoughts like, *If you become afraid, then maybe it could happen! Remember what happened to Job.* It was a ridiculous, vicious cycle: terrible thought, fear, then fear of it coming to pass because I had a fearful thought.

Thank the Lord for His mercy. He helped me to understand through the Scriptures that *Job's* fear was not *my* fear. The fear I was experiencing was nothing more than a passing thought—yet another temptation to fear from the enemy. As long as I refused to entertain that thought, it was not "great" fear.

In reexamining Job 3:25, we see that he *greatly feared*. It was something he thought about all the time. More than likely, he was a chronic worrier. Chronic worrying will open the door for the enemy to bring devastation. Worry is fear at its worst. We don't have to put up with it. We have authority over all the tricks of the enemy. Jesus left His peace on earth with us:

John 14:27
Peace I leave with you, My peace I give to you; not as the world gives do I give to you. Let not your heart be troubled, neither let it be afraid.

Mark 4:37-39

And a great windstorm arose, and the waves beat into the boat, so that it was already filling. But He was in the stern, asleep on a pillow. And they awoke Him and said to Him, "Teacher, do You not care that we are perishing?" Then He arose and rebuked the wind, and said to the sea, "Peace, be still!" And the wind ceased and there was a great calm.

I never realized what an awesome miracle this must have been until I spent three days in the region of the Galilee. Because of the many mountains and frequent weather changes, very seldom is this body of water calm. Even on a clear day, it can be a "tempest in a teapot."

As we quickly approach the times prophesied in the Word of God, it's so comforting to know we have access to the Peace-speaker. No matter what the situation, Jesus is still speaking peace. We can know His peace even in the midst of tragedy and chaos. Now is not the time to fear. We can trust Him when everything around is in turmoil. We must not allow circumstances to determine our destiny. We must lean on the Lord, trust Him for strength, and boldly proclaim His Word to a lost and dying world. There is no safer place than in the center of His will.

Notice the words of the prophet Isaiah spoken several hundred years ago and still resonating with us today:

Isaiah 41:10, 13 (AMPC)

Fear not [there is nothing to fear], for I am with you; do not look around you in terror and be dismayed, for I am your God. I will strengthen and harden you to difficulties...I will help you...I will hold you up and retain you with My [victorious] right hand of rightness and justice...I am the Lord, Who says to you, Fear not; I will help you.

The Church is supposed to be different from the rest of the world, and currently the world is scared stiff. Believers should walk in peace. Let's make sure the lost can easily find their ark of safety because the Church is maintaining its peace and shining a bright light in the midst of great darkness.

The Days of Noah

As in the days of Noah, there's a flood about to come,
A flood of God's judgment will shake the nations.
But there is an Ark of Safety being built right now,
It is the Church of the Lord, filled with Holy Ghost and p'wer.

As in the days of Noah, there is a flood about to come,
A flood of God's glory will sweep the nations.
The Church will rise high as the waters run deep,
The Lord returns for His Bride, forever more to keep.

Build the house, strengthen its beams.
Bring them in piece by piece.
One by one, two by two,
Multitude by multitude.

~A Word from the Lord
January 2001

CONGENITAL BIRTH DEFECT HEALED

Healing Is for All

I was raised in a household that didn't always go to church. My parents didn't start attending services until I was nine years old. I remember that first Sunday morning, watching in amazement as my mother literally ran to the altar to be saved. I didn't understand, but it sure did change things at our house.

I had a similar experience the following spring at the age of 10. I didn't understand what had happened, but I knew I felt a lot better. Something changed inside. The most notable difference was my interest in the Bible. I read it tirelessly from the moment I got saved.

Being young and inquisitive, I had lots of questions. We attended a small denominational church in our community, and I'm certain my sweet Sunday school teacher grew weary of my endless questions in class. I remember one instance like it was yesterday. I had been reading a lot in the New Testament and stumbled across terminology and events in the book of Acts that I didn't understand. We certainly didn't have anything happening like that in our church. I could hardly wait until Sunday morning to ask my teacher about them.

When I asked her about speaking in tongues and healing, her reply wasn't what I expected. "Oh, Honey," she said, "You must *never* read the book of Acts. God never intended for it to be in the Bible. It is of the devil. You must *never* read that book again!" Her statements literally sucked the life out of my zeal for the Word. If the book of Acts was of the devil, then were there other scripture passages that were also unsafe to read?

I stopped reading my Bible. Life with Jesus became about learning and following the rules of my church. The relationship that I had once enjoyed was stifled by my reluctance to venture again into His Word. By the time I was 17, I judged everything and everyone with a "holier than thou" attitude, never having an opportunity to fully grasp the concepts of love and acceptance outlined in the New Testament.

When I was 12, it was discovered that I had a tilted pelvis—a congenital condition from birth. The doctor said that as my body matured it would give me trouble, and he was right. By the time I was 20, I dislocated my hip at least once a month. I could simply walk down the sidewalk and my hip would unexpectedly and painfully pop out of joint. Our family doctor confirmed there was nothing that could be done and that I would have to live with it the rest of my life.

When I entered college, I had problems finding a church I liked. After only a few months, I was completely out of fellowship with God. My lifestyle quickly deteriorated. By the beginning of my second year, I was completely backslidden. It seems like I squeezed a whole life-time of sin into about 19 months. I never felt so alone and unloved in all my life. No matter what I did, I seemed to drift further and further from God.

As time passed, God put people in my path to draw me closer to Him. There were several things that touched me, but my lifestyle didn't immediately change for the better. In January of my junior year, I had a serious car accident, wrapping the car around a telephone pole. Amazingly, I basically walked away without a scratch.

After that, I knew something had to change, but I couldn't forgive myself for straying so far from God. A few weeks later, a family friend sent me a plane ticket to visit him in Florida over spring break. I thought I was going there to have a "good time," but God was setting me up.

First thing upon my arrival, my friend dragged me to church. When I walked in, the people greeted me saying, "Welcome! We love you!" I remember thinking, *If you knew me, you wouldn't love me.* The whole trip was misery for my backslidden soul. Every time I got in the car, the radio would be tuned to a Christian station. There was an overly friendly neighbor lady who seemed to want to go everywhere with us. I thought she was insane because she muttered under her breath all the time. Little did I know, she was a powerful evangelist and great woman of prayer.

After a full week of what seemed like utter torment, I picked a fight with my friend, saying things that hurt him terribly. He walked out, causing me to realize that I had just attacked the one friend who truly cared about me. Broken in spirit, I fell to my knees. Right there in the living room of that home, Jesus came and stood before me. I washed His feet with my tears, rising completely forgiven, cleansed, and changed. I knew I would NEVER be the same.

Yet there was still a lot about that encounter that I didn't understand. It suddenly occurred to me that the friendly neighbor lady down the street would probably be able to explain what had happened to me. So, at 11 o'clock at night, I went skipping down the street to her house. She was wide awake waiting for me.

Her explanation of my experience started in *the book of Acts!* She quickly took me through so many scriptures my head spun. From Acts, she moved on to tell me in detail about healing and speaking in tongues from 1 Corinthians 12 and 14. It didn't take long for my religious upbringing to rear its ugly head. In a very "holier than thou" tone and a "talk to the hand gesture," I firmly explained to her, "*That stuff* is of the devil" and that I didn't want to hear any more of what she had to say. She completely ignored my remark and kept right on pouring the *truth* into my tender heart.

Finally, I could take no more. I hopped out of my seat and started for the door. However, much to my dismay, I was stopped in my tracks. Paralyzed with pain, I was literally stuck in her dining room. Her eyes gleaming with the tangible love of God, she looked at me and said, "What's wrong with you?"

With sarcasm I snarled, "I just dislocated my hip. Want to *heal* me?" God is so merciful. It's a wonder lightning didn't strike me dead.

"I won't heal you, but GOD will!" she answered. Then, quickly rounding the corner (as I made useless efforts to drag myself to the door), she anointed my forehead with oil and placed her hand on my head.

When she touched me, part of me wanted to believe God would be that good. Part of me longed to believe that God was a healing God, but my religious training got the better of me. The long and short of it was that I couldn't fathom the notion that God could be that good. Then, like warm oil pouring down over my head, a prickly sensation washed over every fiber of my being. Starting at the top of my head, the healing power of God poured over my body. When it reached my hip, the pain instantly dropped to my heel and exploded out the end of my toes. Somewhere along the way, damaged cartilage in my ankle was also repaired. From that time to now—30 plus years—I haven't dislocated my hip again or had any problems with that ankle.

I walked away that night knowing in my heart that God truly is a forgiving and loving Father—and that if He would heal me, He would heal anyone. *He got my attention!*

The hallmark scripture of lessons I learned that night is found in John 10:

John 10:10 (KJV)
The thief [the devil] cometh not, but for to steal, to kill, and to destroy: I am come that they might have life, and that they might have it more abundantly.

If anything that happens in our lives is related to theft, death, or destruction, it's not from God. Period. Has the devil stolen your joy? Has your peace of mind been destroyed? Is sickness killing your body? Don't blame God. His desire is for you to experience abundant life.

Thorough study of the Bible over the years has only served to confirm in my heart that most of what I was taught as a child was nothing more than myth and "religious" tradition with no foundation in the whole of Scripture. I have learned that it *is* God's will to heal, just as much as it is His will to save the lost. It's a package deal.

Did you know that the word *savior* has a seven-fold meaning? According to Vine's Expository Dictionary of New Testament Words, the word translated *savior* means *savior, preserver, deliverer, protector, healer, sustainer, used of God.* Receiving Jesus as Lord will not just save you from your sins, God will also heal your body, protect you from harm, and deliver you from all manner of evil—just to name a few of many benefits.

There are literally hundreds of passages in the Bible that explain healing *is* part of our covenant. Healing is part of who God is and what God does. He truly is *that* good.

STOPPING THE FATHER OF LIES

An Eternal God Is Not in the Business of 'Temporary'

W hen I first encountered the healing power of God, it was an entirely new subject for me. I had previously thought that healing was something that only happened to very lucky people—certainly no one in my circles. But once His healing hand was placed upon my life, I somehow knew that if He did it for me, He would do it for anyone.

I remember returning home from Florida feeling changed from the inside out. As a matter of fact, when I walked into my college dorm room, my roommate said, "What happened to you?!"

"What do you mean?" I asked.

"You don't even look like the same person!" she said.

"I'm not," I quietly murmured.

"You're glowing!"

She was right! I wasn't the same person. Words could not express the joy that transformed my heart or the peace that flooded every fiber of my being. I remember so clearly the moment I fell head over heels in love with Jesus. It wasn't when He healed me; that was "icing on the cake." It was when He forgave me. The moment His forgiveness flooded my heart, I made a decision. I knew that I couldn't keep this new-found love to myself. I had to tell others the wonderful *Good News*.

When you know you're forgiven, it rearranges your priorities. It didn't take long for me to decide I would never purposefully do anything to bring reproach to God. I didn't want people to think badly of Him. My lifestyle would have to change drastically if I was going to proclaim His love to others.

The first few weeks back at college were filled with newness and change. He became my first thought when I woke up and the last when I went to bed at night. I turned my back and walked away from the bad influences that had led me down a path of destruction. In some ways, those were lonely days: no friends and nothing to do—just me and Jesus. Yet I wouldn't trade those lonely times for anything. He was right there with me, every step of the way. He made it so easy.

Somewhere in the middle of those tender months of getting to know Him more personally, something alarming was happening to my body. The hip that had been healed started feeling stiff and uncomfortable again much like it would feel before a dislocation. Fear gripped my mind and assaulted me with thoughts: *God didn't really heal you. You're going to dislocate that hip again. Watch out! That healing stuff was just a figment of your imagination. Maybe God did heal you, but it was only temporary.* On and on these kinds of thoughts bombarded my mind. All the while something in my heart said, "No! That's not right. God did heal me. I *know* I experienced the healing power of God. Something is not right, but it's not God's fault."

Even though I didn't actually dislocate my hip again, I experienced strong indications that it could happen at any moment, which perplexed and concerned me. I thought, *If God really healed me, how could this be happening?*

One afternoon sitting in my car in the middle of a parking lot praying in frustration, I turned on the car radio in desperation. Finding a radio station that supported my new lifestyle was a challenge. Christian radio was practically unheard of back then, but there was one station in the area that offered Bible teaching. I tuned in just in time to hear an older gentleman teaching about healing, and my ears perked up. He was talking about how the devil will try to steal your healing after God has touched your body.

I had never heard anything like that before, but it was music to my ears. He mentioned how the devil will lie to us and try to convince us that God didn't really heal us (John 8:44). He explained that Jesus had already defeated Satan, and as Christians, we don't have to put up with the devil or his lying symptoms. Wow! I had never heard anything like that before in my life. Was that really in the Bible?

I got so excited! I switched the radio off and started thumbing through my Bible to find the scriptures he mentioned. It was true! Everything he said really was in the Bible. I could simply resist the symptoms, and they would leave. This was too good to be true, but it was *true*. Right then and there, I took authority over the devil and those symptoms in the name of Jesus. They left immediately and have never returned. A mighty victory was won that day!

Eager to hear more, I switched the radio back on, only to find that the program was over. What a disappointment! I didn't even know the name of the minister who had been teaching. Even though I tried several times, I couldn't find the program again.

A year and a half later, I found myself sitting in a classroom full of hundreds of hungry Bible school students near Tulsa, Oklahoma. We were anxiously waiting for our instructor to begin his first lesson with our class. I didn't think I had ever heard him speak before, even though he was a very famous minister. Yet, when he opened his mouth and said, "Turn in your Bibles with me…," I recognized his voice. His name was Dr. Kenneth E. Hagin, and it was his voice that delivered the truth of God's Word to me many months before.

God had taken me full circle from a parking lot in Indiana to RHEMA Bible Training Center in Oklahoma. I spent the next two years sitting under the teaching of the man who put me on the side of victory. What an opportunity! The radio lesson Brother Hagin had been teaching that spring day was from a sermon he wrote many years earlier called, *How to Keep Your Healing.* (The lesson has been published in mini-book form by the same title and is available still today.) The scripture texts Brother Hagin references in that book are as follows:

Matthew 8:17
*that it might be fulfilled which was spoken by Isaiah the prophet, saying: "He Himself took our **infirmities** and bore our **sicknesses.** "*

Isaiah 53:4
*Surely he has borne our **griefs** [diseases in literal Hebrew], and carried our **sorrows** [in literal Hebrew]…. [brackets mine]*

1 Peter 2:24
who Himself bore our sins in His own body on the tree, that we, having died to sins, might live for righteousness—by whose stripes you were healed.

2 Corinthians 5:17
*Therefore, if anyone is in Christ, he is a new creation: old things are passed away; behold, all things are become **new.** "*

Romans 10:10
*For with the **heart** one **believes** unto righteousness….*

Psalm 107:20
He sent His word and healed them, and delivered them from their destructions.

James 4:7
…Resist the devil and he will flee from you.

An important thing I've come to understand is that when God does a work in our lives—whether spiritual or physical—He intends for it to last. He is not in the business of "temporary" or "half-way." He is an eternal God.

I'm going to end this section by quoting a confession that Brother Hagin mentions at the end of his mini-book. I don't see where I could improve upon what he already said because it's solidly based on God's Word. It worked for me, and I know it will work for you.

"In the name of the Lord Jesus Christ, I exercise authority over this body of mine. Sickness and disease, I refuse to allow you to stay. This body, this house, belongs to God. It is a temple of God. Satan, you have no right to trespass on God's property. Now you get out. You leave my body. I've got authority over you. I know it, you know it, and God knows it. I hold fast to what I have. I'm keeping my healing!"

THE POWER BEHIND OUR AUTHORITY

*I*n recent years, it seems every minister I respect has been strongly given to teachings on love, and after more than 30 years, I'm only beginning to grasp the importance of it. Love is not an option—it's a command. Really, it's the only commandment Jesus gave to the Church:

Mark 12:29-31
Jesus answered... "you shall love the LORD your God with all your heart, with all your soul, with all your mind, and with all your strength.'... 'You shall love your neighbor as yourself.' There is no other commandment greater than these."

Paul further explains in Romans 13:10 that the commandment of loving our neighbor fulfills all the law. Love is the law by which we are to govern our Christian lives—the gauge by which we measure the success of our walk with God.

Over the years, I've heard hundreds of messages on love. The first was *Faith Worketh by Love* by Kenneth Hagin, Jr. If we want our faith to work, we must walk in love toward God and men. Then, next I read *Love the Way to Victory* by Kenneth E. Hagin. He taught us how to walk in forgiveness and stay out of offense—vital factors in living a victorious Christian life. In September of 2003, our precious father in the faith (Brother Kenneth E. Hagin) moved to heaven, but before He left us, the last message he preached was on love.

Now, after years of hearing messages pertaining to this topic, it's time for us to take a step up. It's time to take a step toward being the glorious Church described in Ephesians 5:27, which is a step in the direction of love.

A woman of God I highly respect, Dr. Billye Brim, has candidly shared how God has opened amazing doors for her in Israel. When she questioned the Lord as to how she got to this point, He reminded her of the divine relationships He had placed in her life and how He had required they love each other no matter what. He said success came "because you stayed together and walked in love." She also has shared how the Lord spoke to her many years ago that there were things about faith that He wanted to reveal, but because the body of Christ did not understand love, they were not ready for the revelation. Most recently, I heard a leading minister in the land correlate love to the supernatural manifestations of God. He pointed out that according to 1 Corinthians chapters 12 and 13, love is the key to seeing the gifts of the Spirit in greater manifestation in these last days. Certainly, it is the more excellent way. Without a doubt, we must understand the basic truths of this very important subject, and I can't say it any better than these men and women of God.

No Greater Force

Several years ago, we started a weekly Bible study in our home to provide practical truths to our newfound friends. We wanted to build a foundation on the basics and were led of the Lord to start with a lesson on the authority of the believer. When we study the believer's authority, we must understand that the word *authority* means *delegated power; the right or power to command.*

Brother Hagin often used the illustration of a policeman directing traffic. The officer does not have the power in and of himself to stop oncoming traffic. However, when he steps into the middle of an intersection, drivers will do whatever he commands because the authority to direct traffic was bestowed upon him by the government he represents. In the same way, we as believers have been given authority in the earth through Jesus Christ. All the power of heaven will back us up when we pray according to the Word.

When God created Adam, He intended that Adam be the king of the earth.

Genesis 1:26-28
Then God said, "Let Us make man in Our image...let them have dominion... Then God blessed them, and God said to them,"...fill the earth and subdue it; have dominion...over every living thing that moves on the earth."

God intended for man to be in charge of creation. He was created to rule (Psalm 8:4-8). Adam lost his authority when he sinned. All of Adam's dominion was passed to or usurped by the one whom Paul refers to as "the god of this world" or Satan (1 Corinthians 4:4). Understanding this truth makes it easier to understand why bad things happen in the earth.

The good news is that Jesus was the last or second Adam according to 1 Corinthians 15:22, which says, "For as in Adam all die, even so in Christ all shall be made alive." Jesus defeated death, hell, and the grave when He was raised from the dead. When He paid the price for man's sin on the cross, He won back the authority and dominion that God originally intended for man.

Ephesians 1:18-22

... that you may know ... the riches of the glory of His inheritance ... and what is the exceeding greatness of His power toward us who believe ... which He worked in Christ when He raised Him from the dead and seated Him at His right hand in the heavenly places, far above all principality and power and might and dominion, and every name that is named ... And He put all things under His feet....

Ephesians 2:6

And raised us up together, and made us sit together in the heavenly places in Christ Jesus.

Ephesians chapter one tells of the authority restored in Christ, and chapter two tells us the same authority is available to believers today (Revelation 3:20-21; Ephesians 1:3; Philippians 2:9-11; Colossians 2:9-10, 15).

As I began to study this subject through cross-references, the word *love* began to stand out to me in a way I had never seen before:

John 17:20-26

*[Jesus said praying] "I do not pray for these alone, but also for those who will believe in Me through their word...that they all may be one ... that the world may believe that You sent Me. And the glory which You gave Me I have given them...that they may be made perfect ... that the world may know that You have ... **loved** them as You have **loved** Me. ...that they may behold My glory which You have given Me; for You **loved** Me...that the **love** with which You **loved** Me may be in them, and I in them." [brackets mine]*

In speaking of revealing His glory and power, I began to see Jesus making a strong correlation to the love of God. We can see Paul tie it together even clearer in Romans 8.

Romans 8:37-39

Yet in all these things we are more than conquerors through Him who loved us. For I am persuaded that neither death nor life, nor angels nor principalities nor powers, nor things present nor things to come, nor height nor depth, nor any other created thing, shall be able to separate us from the love of God which is in Christ Jesus our Lord.

As we examine this passage, we can see it's about being more than a conqueror; it's about victory and authority in this life—not just in the life to come. It provides an extensive list of powers or forces in the earth today: death, life, principalities or powers (demonic forces), the present, the future, etc. Whatever the dimension—whatever the creature—there's no force or power greater than the love of God. God's love is the true power behind our authority! It's the power of the Church!

1 John 4:16

And we have known and believed the love that God has for us. God is love, and he who abides in love abides in God, and God in him.

The law of heaven that backs up our authority is the law of love. How often do we ask God to do something for us with less than His love pouring from our hearts? If selfishness, pride, envy, strife or anything of the like are what move us to prayer, how effective can we truly be with the authority that has been bestowed upon us? How often do we go to prayer truly motivated by love? If we want to see the hand of God move in a powerful, supernatural way in this day, we *must* be ever conscious of His love for us and all of mankind.

It has often been said that there's nothing more powerful than a mother's prayers. Why is that? More than likely, it's because a mother's prayers for her children are motivated from a heart of pure, unconditional love.

May it be that we not abuse the power than has been given to us. May it be that after centuries of backbiting and strife, we finally allow the love of God to govern the spiritual laws we've so mechanically learned to operate. If we want to see the glorious Church promised in the Word of God, we *must* step up to *love* in every area of life—especially in prayer.

DEMONS BELIEVE AND TREMBLE

They Tremble Because They Are Afraid

Over the years, several individuals have observed an unusual level of boldness in my praying, especially when it comes to dealing with the devil. Some have inquired as to how I can pray in such a manner. To me it's simply a matter of making my supply of the Spirit (Philippians 1:19) as all believers should. Yet as I sought the Lord, He brought to my remembrance an experience I had when I was very young in Him—an experience that gave me a vivid picture of what the devil really sees when He looks at a Christian.

We're entering in to a time now when we must tell what we know to help one another understand spiritual realities often overlooked or misunderstood, so I am compelled to share the experience. When I had been filled with the Spirit less than six months and long before Bible school, I had an encounter whereby I *know* what demons see when they look at me. I've hesitated to share it over the years because it seems "far out"—maybe even little scary to the natural man. Yet, the knowledge of it has given me a profound boldness in the spirit, and I trust it will do the same for you.

First and foremost, whenever we experience something in the realm of the Spirit, it's important to have scripture to back it up, so let's consider a few important passages.

Philippians 2:9-10
Therefore God also has highly exalted Him and given Him the name which is above every name, that at the name of Jesus every knee should bow, of those in heaven, and of those on earth, and of those under the earth.

Revelation 1:5
...To him that loved us and washed us from our sins in his own blood....

James 2:19 (NLT)
You say you have faith, for you believe that there is one God. Good for you! Even the demons believe this, and they tremble in terror.

Galatians 3:27
For as many of you as were baptized into Christ have put on Christ.

AN UNEXPECTED ENCOUNTER

It was the summer of 1984. My college roommate and I rented an off-campus apartment. It was in a bad neighborhood, but I was so in love with Jesus I hardly noticed. I had received the infilling of the Holy Spirit in March and was so hungry for God I attended church wherever and whenever I could. On this particular night, I had gone with friends to a church in a neighboring state. It was really late when they dropped me off.

My roommate was not at home, so the house was dark. To my surprise, one of her friends was sitting on the front doorstep. As I approached in the darkness, the red glow of the cigarette in her hand alerted me to her presence. We had a quick exchange of greetings and agreed that she should come inside to wait for our mutual friend. I unlocked the door, turned on some lights, and began to prepare for bed. She threw her cigarette into the yard, took a seat in the living room, and five minutes later found her way to my room. She was obviously lonely and needed to talk to someone, so even though I was tired I found a way to be attentive.

I found out after the fact that she had been delving into an Eastern religion and had zealously sought to reach a place they call "nirvana." This place she had achieved was a supposed euphoric state of being. Unfortunately, she did not know what she was getting into or, perhaps I should say, what was getting into her. In actuality, she was possessed by a demonic spirit. In all my years of ministry, she is one of a few individuals I've encountered in such a condition. She had willfully opened herself up to a religious spirit, inviting it to consume her whole existence. When faced with the opportunity to receive Jesus, she rejected Him again and again, instead choosing to cling to the darkness which had overwhelmed her. She had enjoyed it—at least until she decided to drop in for a visit.

As the conversation progressed that night, the young woman discovered that I had just come from church. So, she decided we should talk "religion," even though I had no idea what I was getting into. She talked about God and His love, and it all seemed good right up to point when she began to exhort me regarding the need to love all of God's creation, including Satan. In that moment, the hair stood up on the back of my neck, and I heard myself say to her, "Loving Satan is worshipping him."

As I raised my hand to reject the thought, God's tangible presence enveloped me like an insulated blanket. Simultaneously, the demonic spirit that possessed her realized he had been exposed and began to manifest quite dramatically.

Suddenly mortified, she attempted to stand, but the spirit in her literally picked her up and propelled her airborne backwards across the room. She crashed into the wall, crumpled to the floor, and began whimpering like a dog.

I didn't know what to do. But God! His presence was so strong on me that there was no fear—*absolutely no fear!* An overwhelming sense of peace and love washed over me while she trembled on the floor. I had supernatural compassion for her, knowing that the Lord wanted to set her free. I began praying in the Spirit, knowing that demons have to leave at the mention of His name. She whimpered louder. I raised my hand toward her, but she screamed with her eyes shut tight. I dropped my hand and prayed, and she whimpered. I raised my hand, and she screamed.

This went on for several minutes until she opened her eyes and looked at me. When she did, I saw a change in her eyes. Normally, the color was a light hazel, but at that moment, they were blacker than black. I saw through the window of her soul how utterly lost she was; there was no light within her.

Suddenly, she let out a bloodcurdling scream which raised a real concern that the neighbors would call the police. I stopped praying. She stopped screaming. After a few moments, I resumed praying in the Spirit. She resumed whimpering. It was all very surreal.

Every once in a while, I would mention the name of Jesus, and she would scream as if she were being torn apart. Then she opened her eyes a second time, looked at me, and said with great shame, "Don't look at me! I can't bear to have you look at me." She turned her face away, whimpering. I turned my face away and resumed praying in the Spirit.

Over the course of the evening, she had several opportunities to receive Jesus as her Lord and Savior, but again and again rejected Him. I now understand that she did not want that "feel-good" spirit to leave her. It was her willful choice.

I could have pressed the issue and forced the spirit out of her, but she would have only invited him back. And when he returned, he would have brought more darkness along with him (Matthew 12:43-45; Luke 11:24-26).

"What's your point?" you might be asking. I shared all of this to tell you what happened next.

When I finally ceased praying, eventually the young woman came to herself. The demon inside her stopped manifesting, and she was able to pick herself up off the floor. Trembling, she took a seat nearby.

"What just happened here?" I asked.

"I don't know, but I need help. Don't I?" she answered.

"Yes, you do, and Jesus is here to help you!" Once again, I invited her to know Him personally.

Again, she declined. But with amazing clarity, she began to recall what had happened from her perspective. "It's weird!" she said with a note of disgust. "When I opened my eyes the first time and looked at you, you were covered with blood!" Then she pondered quite reverently, "When I looked at you the second time, Jesus was standing in your place. I couldn't bear to have Him look at me."

Think about what this young woman saw. She saw me covered in the blood of Jesus, which made the demon tremble in fear. She saw Jesus standing in my place! In her darkest moment, Jesus was there to save her. What a tragedy that even in the face of Jesus Christ Himself, she still said no to Him. How could anyone reject that kind of love?

It was the first time I had ever experienced a tangible anointing like that. Every time since then, I am oh so aware that to be clothed with glory is to "put on Christ." When demons see me—or any born-again believer—they see the blood of Christ. And they tremble!

Friends, this is not just about me. This is about *you!* This is about every born-again believer taking his or her place and being clothed with the power of Jesus Christ. If we could only catch a glimpse of all that has been bestowed upon us—the Church, His bride, His body—the devil would not run roughshod over our daily lives or our nation. We would be standing up to him and putting a stop to the demonic forces that plague us.

Frightening things are happening in the earth. But for believers who know who they are in Christ, these things must bow to the name of Jesus. When we take our place in Him, the enemy is defeated at every turn. We don't have authority over the minds and wills of people, but we do have authority over the demonic influences driving them to commit the horrible things they do. There's a power in the name and blood of Jesus that makes the powers of darkness tremble.

2 Timothy 1:7
For God has not given us a spirit of fear, but of power and of love and of a sound mind.

Colossians 2:15 (AMPC)
[God] disarmed the principalities and powers that were ranged against us and made a bold display and public example of them, in triumphing over them in Him and in it [the cross]. [brackets mine]

The battle has been won, but it must be walked out—using His name, His Word, and the authority He has bestowed upon us as believers.

PUT ON CHRIST

Earlier we quoted Galatians 3:27, "For as many of you as have been baptized into Christ have put on Christ" (KJV). Yet, after hearing the account of the demon-possessed young woman, we should have a much deeper understanding of the passage. She saw a believer covered with the blood of Jesus and then experienced the appearance of Jesus Christ Himself standing in my place. Powerful!

At the time, I didn't understand. After all, I was certainly overwhelmed with His presence, but I didn't actually see Him. Frankly, I was uncomfortable telling this story for many years. I thought it had little scripture to back up the experience until the Lord brought me to Galatians 3:27. Then, I clearly understood that the moment in my apartment so many years ago perfectly illustrated the scripture.

I didn't even know the phrase "put on Christ" was in the Bible. I had to look it up. But sure enough, there it was, plain as day. In addition, Romans 13:14 says, "But put ye on the Lord Jesus Christ, and make not provision for the flesh, to fulfil the lusts thereof." If we tend to let our minds dwell upon our own sinful nature, this line of thinking can be overwhelming. Who do we think we are?

Yet, here's the truth of the matter. I was a sinner, but now I am saved by grace. God no longer sees a sinner when He looks at me. He sees me in Him and calls me a saint whether I feel like one or not. What about you?

On a few occasions since that day, I've been in church services where I was keenly aware of Jesus moving through the crowd, looking for those who would be willing to *put on Christ*. If we'll ever be who He has called us to be—one *in* Him, glorified *in* Him, perfected *in* Him, and seated *with* Him in heavenly places—we must change the way we think about ourselves as believers and understand the way He sees us *in Him*.

A SEASON OF WAITING & WATCHING

The Harvester's Dilemma

I know I'm not alone wondering what's happening in the world today. Many in the body of Christ have shared their dismay regarding the times in which we're living—times when direction from the Lord seems scarce but encouragement abounds. It seems the Lord is providing very few specifics about the coming days but instead speaking words of blessing over us. It's almost as if we're operating strictly on a "need to know" basis. So, we should understand that Jesus is coming soon. I think a large portion of the Christian world perceives there's a huge influx of believers about to be birthed into the kingdom, but for now, we wait and watch.

Don't get me wrong. The work of the Lord is still going forth in the earth. There are many, especially those on the foreign mission field, who already are running with vision and divine purpose. Yet, for the most part, those of us in the United States wait.

THE FARMER

Let us consider the farmer for a moment. Having grown-up an authentic Midwest farmer's daughter, I understand a few things about the elements of farming—plowing, planting, cultivating, and harvest. Springtime is a busy time of year with ground preparation and planting. The farmer works hard during this season, not really resting until the seed is in the ground. From then on, he watches. He watches young plants for an overgrowth of weeds, and thus, he cultivates. He watches the weather and waits, for much of the process of growing is out of his hands at that point. Nature must take its course, and much of what concerns him must be left in the hands of God.

Eventually, there comes a time in the growing season when the cultivating is over, and the farmer prepares for what comes next. It is a time when he grows anxious and uncomfortable knowing the biggest task is ahead of him. His preparations might include servicing machinery or increasing capacity to store the harvest. Ultimately, when harvest time comes, it's "all hands-on deck." There will be no rest until the harvest is in. A true farmer hardly sleeps during this season. It's a full-on press to bring in the grain from the field. Harvest time is a very joyous time, but for the serious farmer, he seldom grants himself the luxury of resting or celebrating until his work is done.

Isaiah 40:27-31

Why do you say, O Jacob, and speak, O Israel: "My way is hidden from the LORD, and my just claim is passed over by my God"? Have you not known? Have you not heard? The everlasting God, the LORD, the Creator of the ends of the earth, neither faints nor is weary. His understanding is unsearchable. He gives power to the weak, and to those who have no might He increases strength. Even the youths shall faint and be weary, and the young men shall utterly fall, But those who wait on the LORD shall renew their strength; they shall mount up with wings like eagles, they shall run and not be weary, they shall walk and not faint.

If we find ourselves in a position of waiting, we should rejoice and understand that God in His great mercy is giving us opportunity to rest, grow, and prepare. If we'll properly yield to the opportunity, our strength will be renewed. We'll mount up with wings like eagles, and we'll develop the stamina to run without becoming weary or fainting. If we don't take time now to wait upon the Lord and rest in Him, the days ahead might be too much for us. For when it's time, harvest must come in quickly.

James 5:7-8

Therefore be patient, brethren, until the coming of the Lord. See how the farmer waits for the precious fruit of the earth, waiting patiently for it until it receives the early and latter rain. You also be patient. Establish your hearts, for the coming of the Lord is at hand.

Even though the farmer is anxious for the harvest to come, he hovers over his crops until they are fully ripe. It should be the same with us. We should hover over the coming harvest with prayer—and lots of it. What could possibly be more important while we wait?

"Prayer for what?" someone might ask. You name it! Pray for the lost, for resources, for laborers, for weather, and for whatever the Lord puts upon your heart. Yield to His direction and pray. Pray with your understanding and pray in the Spirit (1 Corinthians 14; Romans 8:26-27).

1 Corinthians 3:6

I have planted, Apollos watered, but God gave the increase.

It's in the growth season of watching and waiting that God brings the increase. What is God doing? He's creating an atmosphere where He can move and the lost will find their way. John 14:6 tells us that Jesus is the way, the truth, and the life.

Psalm 126:5-6

Those who sow in tears shall reap in joy. He who continually goes forth weeping, bearing seed for sowing, shall doubtless come again with rejoicing, bringing his sheaves with him.

Remember, in the season of waiting and watching the most important things that happen are rest, growth, and preparation. The opportunity to be laborers in His harvest will soon be upon us. The important part now is to make certain we're ready.

I THINK MYSELF HAPPY

For many years now, I've taught that *happiness* is a state of mind, whereas *joy* is a spiritual force. Even though joy is a significant component in our spiritual lives, we must not overlook the value of happiness. In examining the subject, our society has a much different perspective of what makes one happy as compared to what the Bible teaches.

A simple word study in the original Hebrew and Greek languages reveals some interesting definitions to the words often translated as *happy*. According to Strong's Exhaustive Concordance, the Hebrew provides the following insights: "*blessed, tranquil, secure, successful, prosper, to be in safety.*" The Greek adds these shades of meaning: "*supremely blessed, fortunate, well off.*" Therefore, to be happy carries the connotation that one has a strong sense of safety and security along with being supremely blessed in every area of life. The Amplified Bible consistently defines *blessed* as "*happy, fortunate, to be envied.*"

Scripturally, there are several ways or areas where we can find happiness in our lives. Let's take a moment to examine them.

Happiness can be simply found by partaking of or providing a *heritage* for one's family in the fear of the Lord.

Psalm 127:3-5
Behold, children are a heritage from the LORD, THE FRUIT OF THE WOMB IS *a reward. Like arrows in the hand of a warrior, So are the*

---

*children of one's youth. **Happy is** the man who has his quiver full of them....*

Psalm 128:1-4

Blessed is every one who fears the LORD, Who walks in His ways.

*When you eat the labor of your hands, you **shall be** happy, and it shall be well with you. Your wife shall be like a fruitful vine in the very heart of your house, your children like olive plants All around your table. Behold, thus shall the man be blessed Who fears the LORD.*

Happiness is also a by-product of walking in *wisdom* and *understanding.*

Proverbs 3:13, 16-18

Happy *is the man who finds wisdom, and the man who gains understanding; Length of days is in her right hand, in her left hand riches and honor. Her ways are ways of pleasantness, and all her paths are peace. She is a tree of life to those who take hold of her, and **happy** are all who retain her.*

If we want happiness, wisdom and understanding are excellent ways to get it.

Proverbs 4:7

Wisdom is the principal thing; Therefore get wisdom. And in all your getting, get understanding.

How do we obtain these things? We can't go to the store and buy them.

James 1:5

If any of you lacks wisdom, let him ask of God, who gives to all liberally and without reproach, and it will be given to him.

Of course, God's Word is filled with wisdom and understanding if we'll take the time to study it. However, these things also come by prayer. James 4:2 says, "We have not because we ask not" (KJV).

Ephesians 1:15-18

Therefore I... do not cease to give thanks for you, making mention of you in my prayers: that the God of our Lord Jesus Christ, the Father of glory, may give to you the spirit of wisdom and revelation in the knowledge of Him, the eyes of your understanding being enlightened; that you may know what is the hope of His calling....

2 Chronicles 9:7

Happy are your men and happy are these your servants, who stand continually before you and hear your wisdom!

For those in leadership, the more a leader walks in wisdom, the more blessed are those who are called alongside to help him or her. They are blessed (happy, fortunate, to be envied) simply by being around the wisdom that proceeds from those in a godly position of authority.

Proverbs 16:20

*He that heeds the word wisely will find good, and whoever trusts in the Lord, **happy** is he.*

There is wisdom in trusting God, and it brings happiness and blessing. *Trust* is a word often used in defining *faith*. In fact, walking in faith is another way to find true happiness.

Romans 10:17

So then faith comes by hearing, and hearing by the word of God.

The simple act of building our faith through the Word of God will automatically help build happiness in our lives. Again, the more time we spend in the Word, the happier we are—more secure, more prosperous, more peaceful, and supremely blessed.

Another thing that brings happiness is simply feeling good about ourselves, especially if we know we're *doing something worthwhile*.

Proverbs 14:21

He that despises his neighbor sins; But he who has mercy on the poor, **happy** *is he.*

When we pastored, our little church was involved in grocery relief program to help feed the hungry. Even though it took nearly the entire congregation to get the job done each month, it brought such happiness to everyone. We were never so happy as on distribution day when hundreds of local families would file through our doors to receive their portion. It really was a beautiful thing.

Proverbs 29:18 (KJV)

Where there is no vision, the people perish: but he that keepeth the law, **happy** *is he.*

There's a sense of accomplishment when we know we're doing the right thing. In the above scripture, isn't it interesting that "keeping the law" and being "happy" are coupled together with "vision"? There's a sense of purpose in following a plan—specifically, the plan of God. When we know we're in the right place at the right time doing the right thing with the right people, there's a strong sense of fulfillment. Regardless of the circumstances, we can happily endure much hardness if we know we have a purpose.

Psalm 144:15

...Happy are the people, **whose God is the LORD.**

By worldly standards, the Israelites (Jews) are undoubtedly the most despised people on the face of the earth. Why is that? They are envied because they are blessed. God prospers whatever they do. No matter how bleak their situation, they just keep surviving and thriving, glorifying God in the process. In the midst of all their trials, persecutions, and sufferings, we find singing and dancing or displays of happiness. They are happy under the most desperate of circumstances.

Psalm 146:5
Happy is he who has the God of Jacob for his help, whose hope is in the LORD his God.

The Jews possess an eternal expectation of blessing because their God is the Lord. If they can maintain happiness in the bleakest of situations, what does that say for us? Actually, it

The apostle Paul is an excellent example. He sets the standard for being happy regardless of his circumstances. In Acts 25 we find Paul's missionary journeys came to an abrupt end at Jerusalem. To avoid death as a Roman citizen, Paul appealed to Caesar. Subsequently taken by heavily armed guards to Caesarea, Paul was sent to appear before Governor Felix. After hearing his case, Felix left him in prison for *two years* for fear of the Jews (still within the borders of his own country). When Felix was replaced by Festus, Paul once again was given an opportunity to speak before he was sent to Rome. This time his case was before King Agrippa:

Acts 26:2
*I think myself **happy**, King Agrippa, because today I shall answer for myself before you concerning all the things of which I am accused of the Jews.*

There are a lot of things Paul could have said in that moment. Yet even though Paul was under intense scrutiny, he was able to find good in the matter. He had a sense of destiny with a knowing that only God could have brought him to this place. He did not focus on the conditions of his captivity, but rather spoke of the happiness in his heart for the opportunity to speak before the king.

To some, it may have looked like Paul was not living a "victorious Christian life." I beg to differ. He had purpose and vision. He was happy! It's important that we keep our thoughts focused on the vision of our hearts. If we magnify adverse circumstances, we'll slip right into the muck and mire of it all, but if we remain focused on the plan, we can be happy regardless of circumstances. God will get the glory for it.

James 5:7-8, 11 (KJV)

*Be patient therefore, brethren, unto the coming of the Lord. Behold, the husbandman waiteth for the precious fruit of the earth, and hath long patience for it, until he receive the early and latter rain. Be ye also patient; stablish your hearts: for the coming of the Lord draweth nigh...Behold, **we count them happy which endure....***

As the coming of the Lord draws near, today's believers qualify as ones enduring to the end of all things. Along with Jesus, they are anticipating the harvest of the precious fruit of the earth. They are not just waiting, but laboring in the harvest.

1 Peter 4:14 (KJV)

If ye be reproached for the name of Christ, happy are ye; for the spirit of glory and of God resteth upon you: on their part he is evil spoken of, but on your part he is glorified.

Again, it's important to maintain the proper focus in every situation. Steadfastly gaze upon the vision, the plan, and the purpose. We must never lose sight of our destiny. If we find ourselves in the middle of adverse circumstances, we must not magnify them. But rather, we must know God's glory rests upon us.

I think myself happy! And you?

OBSCENE PHONE-CALLER ARRESTED

By the Love of God

Romans 8:38-39

For I am persuaded that neither death, nor life, nor angels nor principalities nor powers, nor things present nor things to come, nor height nor depth, nor any other created thing, shall be able to separate us from the love of God which is in Christ Jesus our Lord.

John 3:16

For God so loved the world that He gave His only begotten Son, that whoever believes in Him should not perish but have everlasting life.

The winter of 1984-85 was probably one of the most pivotal times of my life. While finishing my senior year of college, I was seeking the Lord diligently regarding His plan for my life. It was a time of tremendous spiritual growth as my heart was consumed with zeal and love for my Savior.

I lived off-campus in a fully furnished apartment. The elderly owner provided almost everything needed, including an old telephone that sat on a small table across the room from the bed. One snowy winter night, I was awakened out of a deep sleep by the phone's obnoxiously loud ring. If I remember correctly, the clock read 2:13 a.m. Disoriented, I stumbled out of bed and fumbled for the phone in pitch-black darkness. The next few moments are forever imprinted in my mind.

As I answered the phone, a male voice on the other end began speaking things too inappropriate to repeat. *Is this an obscene phone call?* I wondered. I stood there dazed, still trying to find the answer to that question when he abruptly finished. I thought, *Good. He's done, and now I can go back to bed.*

I started to hang up when I heard in my spirit, "Don't do that!" Before I could even think about those words, I heard myself say, "Do you know that Jesus Christ loves you more than you can ever imagine?" Instinctively, I waited to hear the click of the receiver on the other end of the line, but the *click* never came.

"Hello? Are you there?" I asked, thinking I missed hearing him hang up.

Slowly and softly, a shaking voice on the other end on the line said, "I'm so sorry. I'm so sorry," trailing off into silence.

From there God gave me the awesome opportunity to share the gospel with this absolute stranger. He repented of his sins and asked Jesus to save him right then and there. The love of God had stopped him in his tracks and arrested him from sliding further into the sin that held him captive.

The sun was coming up by the time we ended our conversation about the Lord and His Word. This young man in his early twenties had dialed my number at random. All he knew of me was my first name, which I had given him in the course of conversation. He provided me with his full name, address, and telephone number. For the next several weeks, I had the privilege of helping him find a good church as well as praying with him regarding the many issues in his life.

A few years later, I came to understand a truth that still rings with profound wisdom today: Sinners don't need to be told they're in sin. They already know it. They need to know they are loved.

What an awesome transformation takes place in our lives the moment we realize that God truly loves us. Once we understand that He loves us despite our sin, it's almost impossible to resist the precious gift of Jesus. It's this simple message that we should share in word or in deed with everyone we have the opportunity of knowing or meeting.

TELEMARKETING AND THE PET PEEVE

During the early years of our marriage, my husband and I worked for a ministry based in Oklahoma. We worked and attended church there, and most of our friends were fellow church members or employees of that ministry. Very seldom did we get an opportunity to have fellowship outside of our environment. Not that we didn't love the people, but eventually my heart began to cry out for more. I longed to be able to minister to the lost in my day-to-day life.

In fact, let's "get real." When we're young, it sometimes takes a while to understand how this "love-walk" thing is supposed to work. It's a lifestyle we should all be perfecting until Jesus comes. Yet, to be honest, I used to have one terrible "pet peeve." I hated phone solicitations. They always seemed to call right at dinner time or just as we were about to do something important with family. Many times, I wasn't nice in my dealings with them.

One day as I was praying about my desire to minister to the lost, I heard the following words loud and clear in my heart: "I send people to your home on a regular basis that you could be ministering to, but instead you rudely hang up on them." Ouch!

I adjusted my attitude in a hurry! The next several times we received phone solicitations, I listened very politely to what the callers had to say and then gently asked them to listen to what I had to say about the

Lord. You know, it's odd, but it didn't take very long for those solicitation calls to stop coming to our house.

What am I saying? Let's not limit God by having preconceived ideas of the people to whom we should minister. There are billions of lost people everywhere we turn. Isn't it time we take advantage of *every* opportunity the Lord brings our way? His love is big enough and strong enough to reach the lost all over the world. God's love is the one thing that will get their attention.

A JOYFUL SEASON OF HARVEST

Has the Time Passed for Joy in the body of Christ?

*I*n 1992, the minister for whom we worked started the year off by saying, "'92 is the year for you." I had no idea what all that would entail, but I believed he had heard from the Lord. I believed if we pressed in to the things of God, we would see the extraordinary. In February of that same year, I was amazed when the circles where we fellowshipped began to experience revival like I had never seen or imagined. It was a revival of the joy of the Lord and was the most astonishing thing I've ever witnessed. Like a rushing mighty wind, the Holy Spirit poured Himself into our offices, our cars, our homes, and our church services, filling our hearts with overwhelming joy.

1 Peter 1:8

…yet believing, you rejoice with joy inexpressible and full of glory.

While Pentecostal old-timers had seen this type of move of the Spirit, most of us were like little birds that had never before seen rain. We got in in the presence of God, looked upward, and nearly became overcome by the deluge of joy that flooded our hearts and minds. Nevertheless, it was time! The Church, the body of Christ as a whole, had become dry and barren and needed a deluge—a flood—of God's glory that would take us to a higher place in Him.

2 Corinthians 3:18

But we all, with unveiled face, beholding as in a mirror the glory of the Lord, are being transformed into the same image from glory to glory....

Something changed in our hearts. We moved up to a new level of God's glory. There had been the charismatic revival of the 1970s when God restored the Baptism of the Holy Spirit to large portions of the body of Christ. In the 1980s a revival of teaching swept across the nation, restoring the importance of faith and the Word of God. Neither of these moves stirred up the controversy that surrounded this revival of joy. Some thought it was "ignorance gone to seed," so to speak. Some thought it was "the flesh" running amok. Yet, when all was said and done, no one could deny the change that had come to our hearts because of this overwhelming joy.

What made this move of God so different? We laughed! A lot. The very religious folks thought it was irreverent to laugh in church. Yet because the Holy Spirit inspired it, it was actually a move of God, and what God did in our lives through it was a holy thing.

Romans 14:17

*For the kingdom of God is...righteousness and peace, and **joy** in the Holy Ghost.*

Joy works in many ways, but let's consider one illustration in particular. Think for a moment about a rotten tooth that causes so much pain it affects every part of life until it is fixed. Suppose the dentist says it must come out; then most likely he will use a medicine to numb the area to pain. Some dentists even use what's commonly called "laughing gas." Once the patient is under the influence of the anesthetic, the dentist is able to remove the rotten tooth with minimal pain to the patient.

I believe this is precisely what God was accomplishing during the outpouring of joy. God helped His children overcome past hurts or sin that caused great pain. He was dealing with decay in our souls such as unforgiveness and bitterness. As the Holy Spirit overwhelmed us with joy, we laughed and laughed. When the laughter stopped, those rotten things had been removed—plucked from our hearts and minds by God Himself. He forever changed us by the power of His joy.

This move of God was not without its problems. As with anything, there will always be people who will take things to an extreme. Not long into this precious outpouring, all sorts of excesses cropped up. Some churches spent all their time laughing. They neglected the teaching of the Word and people got off into doctrinal ditches. This type of thing made many ministers nervous. Some began to shy away from allowing the Holy Spirit to move at all in their services. Many breathed a sigh of relief when people stopped laughing and got "serious" about the things of God.

Psalm 126:1-2
When the LORD brought back the captivity of Zion, we were like those who dream. Then our mouth was filled with laughter, and our tongue with singing. Then they said among the nations, "The LORD has done great things for them."

For those of us who witnessed the restoration of joy, the above passage has a special place in our hearts. When God sets one free—joy, laughter, and singing should abound. Now that we've moved into the new millennium, there are many searching for the next move of God. Many have said the next great move of God will be a restoration of the miraculous and then a harvest of souls where great multitudes will be saved.

Let us not get so caught up in looking for the new that we forget the things we've seen and learned from the past. We have not ceased to have a need for the Baptism of the Holy Spirit, have we? Is the Word of God still to be the focal point of our teaching? Is it possible to please God without faith? We still have need of all these things just as the body of Christ still needs regular outpourings of joy.

James 5:7

Therefore be patient, brethren, until the coming of the Lord. See how the farmer waits for the precious fruit of the earth, waiting patiently for it until it receives the early and latter rain.

The above passage is all about harvest—perhaps the "great" harvest for which so many are now looking. God longs to receive the precious fruit of the earth—the souls of mankind coming into the saving knowledge of the Lord Jesus Christ.

Psalm 126:5-6

Those who sow in tears shall reap in joy. He who continually goes forth weeping, bearing seed for sowing, shall doubtless come again with rejoicing, bringing his sheaves with him.

The same Psalm we referenced earlier about joy is also about harvest. It doesn't take a rocket scientist to see they go hand in hand. Having been raised on a farm, I can certainly attest to the fact that harvest time is the most exciting and joyful time of the year. It's the time when the farmer reaps the full benefit of his labor. I don't believe it was by chance that God chose to restore joy to the body of Christ in the last decade of the previous century or millennium. Some may think that this "joy thing" has passed and God has moved on to the next big thing.

Yet, God does not restore blessings and tools to the body of Christ only for them to be lost or swallowed up in the next phase of glory. No, the things He has restored are vitally important in order to move on. We don't get to leave anything out. When it comes to harvest, we need the Holy Spirit, we need His Word, we need the God-kind of faith, and we need His joy.

Folks, its harvest time! If we've lost our joy, will we have the strength we need to do our part in the harvest?

Nehemiah 8:10
...the joy of the LORD is your strength.

Ha! Ha! Ha!

HARVEST RIPE FOR PICKING

Eternal Work Produces Fruit That Remains

John 15:16 (KJV)
Ye have not chosen me, but I have chosen you, and ordained you, that ye should go and bring forth fruit, and that your fruit should remain....

*W*hen the time of fairs and festivals comes around each year, I'm reminded of an encounter that forever changed my perspective of *the harvest.* Many years ago, when I was very young in the ministry, God did something so amazing I could hardly fathom the goodness of His great love.

As I share the following story, it will be sadly obvious that I lacked wisdom and compassion. Thank God for His mercy! He is so patient in teaching us about the depth of His affection. I'm still learning. How about you? I'm certain I'm not the only one God uses despite "stinkin' thinkin'."

Before going to Bible school in the mid-1980s, I did whatever I could to minister in my local area, often singing in small churches or at community events. Every spring our city had a weekend festival with an open-air gospel sing on Sunday. It was attended by hundreds of people—sinner and saint alike. One year, the coordinator had been adamant regarding the schedule. She wanted me to sing later in the evening, specifically requesting me to give an altar call because there would be more people in the park at that time. Because of the large number of participants, my presentation was limited to 15 minutes. I was apprehensive as I thought about speaking. *What would I say?* I wondered.

The day of the event brought beautiful weather. I had been to the park earlier in the afternoon to hear some friends sing, but I was horrified to discover secular carnival booths had been set up right next to the amphitheater. For most of the afternoon an annoying carnival worker rode through the open-air theater on a bicycle with an over-sized boom box playing hard rock music *loudly*. It was a terrible distraction to the audience and the musicians.

Not only did I have anxiety over presenting an altar call for a large crowd, but I realized I would be competing with the threat of this awful carnie and his boom box. It made me mad!

Since the schedule put me at the park so late, there was just enough time to go to a Sunday evening service. While at church, the man on the bicycle became a personal matter of prayer. It went something like this: "God, I don't like that loud carnie interrupting things. I don't like that at all. I'll be trying to minister to people, so I want You to make him stop. I don't want him riding through there when I'm singing. I bind you, Satan, in the name of Jesus...." On and on my prayer went.

Then God had something to say. Ever so gently, God spoke in my heart, "If you will let Me, I'll use you to save him." I was shocked! It was hard to believe that God would want to use me for such a task—especially given my poor attitude. God's agenda was completely different than mine. When God looked at the situation, He saw a lost soul riding a bicycle and crying out for help. Moved to prayer once more, I gave myself over to heart-felt intercession for this young man's soul. I left the time of prayer different from when I had begun.

Calmly returning to the park, the altar call I had agonized over for days became much clearer. Honestly, I don't remember what songs were sung. I don't really remember what words were spoken. I opened my mouth, and God filled it. The invitation was made for anyone "within the sound of my voice" to ask the Lord into his or her heart. I gave simple instructions for those who would respond to meet me behind the amphitheater for prayer. No one came. I was disappointed, and I assumed I must have missed God.

Others got up to sing while I returned to my seat in the audience dejected. But much to my surprise, the program emcee asked me to return to the platform. She said there were some young men backstage who wanted to talk to me. *Me?*

I looked up in utter astonishment! Standing backstage were the carnie and two of his buddies. They had come to ask Jesus into their hearts. My heart skipped a beat and felt as if it jumped into my throat.

Numb and almost speechless, I approached them. Even though I had previous experience leading others to the Lord, I felt ill prepared for this moment. It was dark, and they were much dirtier than I had anticipated. But we surely can't let a little darkness or a little dirt get between others and God, so I pressed on with a quick greeting.

A brief conversation confirmed that they did indeed want to be saved. So, we prayed the sinner's prayer together, and Jesus came into their hearts. It was precious! It's amazing how lives can be changed forever in a moment of time.

I recall one of the men seemed a little older than the others. It didn't take long to determine that he might have been somewhat mentally delayed. His speech was simple. His personal hygiene needed serious attention. His white T-shirt was brown, and his teeth were green. His breath turned my stomach. Yet, the Lord urged me on.

After some instruction from the Word, these new believers were invited to be filled with the Holy Spirit. The older fellow said, "You know, I think I could do that."

"Go ahead, brother!" was my reply. He instinctively raised his hands into the air and began to pray in a language he did not know or understand. It was one of the most beautiful things I have ever heard. To this day, I cry when I think about it. The others soon joined in.

God miraculously saved and filled those unlearned, previously unclean men with the Holy Spirit. I walked away dwarfed by the unconditional and unchanging love of God.

Several years later, we were visiting with family in that same city and had stopped at a fast-food restaurant for lunch. The place was packed. They were so busy they had placed some of the kitchen staff out front to take orders while customers waited in line. One of the gentlemen clearly had some personal hygiene issues, and the business-side of me wondered what management had been thinking when they put him in full view of the general public.

When it was our turn to order, this same man stepped up to me and said rather slowly, "I like your shirt!" which referenced something about Jesus. In the very next instant, my mind flashed back to that lovely spring evening in the park some 12 years earlier when the carnies asked Jesus into their hearts. In my mind's eye, I could see the man with the green teeth and the beautiful prayer language. Suddenly, I realized it was him! Gulp.

There he was, standing before me just as he had that night long ago, still loving Jesus. This man was no longer simple. He was older and much cleaner, his teeth no longer green. He no longer lived the carnie life, having put down roots in the same city where he had found his Savior. Watching him interact with the people was a joy. He shared the love of God with whomever would listen—even with those who were too busy to notice what a treasure Jesus had found.

I found something, too, that blustery December day—*fruit that remained.*

Proverbs 11:30
The fruit of the righteous is a tree of life; and he who wins souls is wise.

Isaiah 3:10
Say to the righteous that it shall be well with them, for they shall eat the fruit of their doings.

Hasten to the Harvest

Listen, listen, listen
The sound of the trumpet of God.
The chariots, the horsemen and riders
The day is at hand.
Time to draw near.
Listen and you will hear.
Spirit and truth
Time to move
Hasten to the harvest.

Press in, press in to the fullness of God
For equipping and warfare like never before.
The battle's been won, but it must be walked out.
I'm returning, I'm returning – Released with a shout
Never more to be separated from my beloved Church.
There are days of heaven to be seen upon earth.

So move with the Spirit.
Flow in the groove.
There's an anointing, so just move.
Anointing to harvest
Anointing to reap
Anointing to set captives free.
Hasten. Do not delay.
The harvest must come in quickly.
Pray, pray, pray.

Word from the Lord
May 5, 1997

TWO IMPORTANT DECISIONS

Hearing from God and Being Led by His Spirit

After my "Saul-on-the-road-to-Damascus-experience" in Florida in 1984, my life was forever changed. When I first returned to Indiana and college, I wanted to quit school and go into ministry. I really didn't know where to begin. I felt strongly that God wanted me to finish my business degree since I only had a little over a year left at the university. So, in the next year and half apart from my school work, I spent all my extra time developing as a believer and pressing full-on into the plan of God.

One of the most blessed things the Lord did for me during that time was to place me in a small weekly Bible Study taught by a woman I had never met before. It was there that I learned about growing up spiritually. It was there that the teacher poured into us the subject about which she was most passionate—prayer. It took me years to realize the massive impact this woman had upon my spiritual development as a believer and future five-fold ministry calling. This very gifted teacher, also an editor and writer, went on to become a Christian publisher—in fact, my publisher and the publisher of *this* book. I cannot thank God enough for the wonderful work He did in my heart and life through her gifts.

When graduation from college was looming, it was decision time. What came next? I spent a significant quantity of time with my teacher learning about how to follow the plan of God. She recommended some materials: a book by Dr. Kenneth E. Hagin titled, *How You Can Be Led by the Spirit of God,* and an audio teaching series by Rev. Mark Brazee, *How You Can Know the Will of God.* (Those materials or similar ones are still available today through their respective ministry websites and still highly recommended by this student.)

It was during this season that this verse in Hebrews 4 became real to me:

Hebrews 4:12
For the word of God is quick, and powerful, and sharper than any twoedged sword, piercing even to the dividing asunder of soul and spirit, and of the joints and marrow, and is a discerner of the thoughts and intents of the heart.

Rev. Brazee explained that the Word of God can help us divide our own thoughts from God's thoughts. If we'll double up on the Word, it will chisel away our own thinking and allow the plan of God to rise up from our hearts.

That's what I did. I doubled up on the Word. I was so new to the things of God that I really was not certain *what* passages to read. So, I just stuck with something I knew to be "safe"—1 Corinthians 13, the love chapter. I read it over and over and over again. Then one day, while having lunch with my teacher, she suggested, "Why don't you go to RHEMA?" I had never heard that word *rhema* before in my life. I didn't know what it was. I didn't know anything about it. But the moment she said those words, something exploded in my belly, and suddenly, I knew that I knew that I knew that RHEMA was God's plan for me.

Right then and there, I made the first most important decision of my career—to go to Bible school. However, this major decision called for a move to a place I had never been to before and to study from people I had never heard of or met before. Yet, to this day I've never regretted that decision because it was born in the heart of God. We simply found it there hidden in my heart—placed there by God from the beginning, even though I didn't know about it until that moment.

Two years later and a graduate of one of the most prestigious Bible schools in the world, I found myself with a burning call to the nations and once again seeking direction for my "next steps" from the Master. Actually, the direction was pretty clear, but not at all what I wanted to hear. God was sending me back to the city from whence I came. For the life of me, I could not fathom what this could possibly have to do with going to the nations and tried my best to talk God out of it. I gave Him all sorts of conditions I wanted to be met before I would accept the assignment. Of course, God inevitably refused to meet a single condition. He expected me to walk by faith without complaint or argument.

His admonition to me was, "Peter didn't walk on the water until He got out of the boat." Ouch and hallelujah all at the same time! So, I got out of the boat and returned to Indiana in reverential obedience.

I will also add that I was thoroughly disappointed that I graduated from Bible school single. I had hoped I would find my lifetime companion in Bible school. What better place to meet a man of God, I had reasoned. Yet, approximately three months after my return to Indiana, I heard myself tell a friend, "I don't care if I ever get married. Jesus is enough for me. If He wants me to remain single the rest of my life, I'm okay with that." I was truly content doing the will of God. Then six weeks later, I met the man that I would eventually marry.

My future husband attended the same church and was in the choir with me. As the music department was preparing for the annual Christmas program, the director asked me to do the set design, which was a long-forgotten bullet-point on my resume. This super-quiet guy was assigned to help me build it. We worked well together throughout the entire season. I didn't give him any serious consideration because I assumed that he was fresh out of high school.

We started out as friends, and I found myself sort of liking him. But repeatedly, I dismissed the idea of anything more than friendship because of the assumed age difference. I had almost come to the point of giving up my concerns until one day in conversation I discovered we were the same age. That was pretty much it. I knew I was in love.

Bryan Shaw did not strike me as the kind of guy who wanted to go anywhere but *home*. "What about the nations, Lord?" I asked in prayer. Our first few weeks of dating were one long, hard-fought battle in prayer because this guy did not fit into the mold I thought I needed in a husband. My first "but God!" was met with this word from the Father: "Be still when you are with him. Look in your heart and find the peace and joy I have placed there. Follow peace" (Isaiah 55:12).

For those of us who have the privilege of knowing Bryan, we know him to be a man of great peace. There was a season in the early years of our marriage where we worked for one of the leading ministries in the world. He started out vacuuming carpets. All the departments in the ministry fussed with each other about who got the privilege of having Bryan vacuum their little corner of the world. It was reported back to me that, "When Bryan walks in the room, he brings peace with him." They all wanted his peace to rest in their departments. But I get to have his peace rest in our home every minute of every day.

My second "but God!" had to do with my question about the nations. The Lord's answer broke my heart. He said, "I want you to give that call back to me. If it's of Me, I'll give it back to you when it's time." It truly was the hardest thing I've ever done. It was so painful, in fact, that our children never knew their mother even had a call to the nations. We raised them to adulthood without them ever knowing because it was just too painful for me to speak about it.

The final "but God!" was met with this admonition from the Lord: "I'm giving him to you as a precious and valuable gift. Treasure the gift!" We were engaged six weeks after our first date and married seven months later. Of the major decisions of my life, it was the second but most important.

Now, for the rest of the story. Between 2003 and 2014 we pastored a church in small-town America. In 2011, the Lord began dealing with me that we would be leaving the pastorate to return to itinerate ministry. Then in June of 2014, He required us to resign our positions and leave the community we had served faithfully for 11 years. There was a lot about that departure that we did not understand at the time, but we obeyed. We then took a sabbatical for 13 months to regroup and find center.

In December of 2014, I had a profound visitation from the Lord. It lasted but for a moment—just long enough to receive a word from Him that shook me to the very center of my being. He said, "I am about to send you to the many nations of the earth. You will return and report all that you have seen and heard. Heal the sick! Raise the dead!"

Then in January of the following year, approximately five weeks later, I found myself standing on the side-walk in front of "Glorious Way Church" in Houston, Texas. It was in that moment I felt the breath of the Holy Spirit. He whispered, "I gave it back to you." Stunned, it took me only a moment to understand what He meant. Upon my return home, I checked my journal from 1988, and it was 27 years to the day He chose to remind me about the call to the nations and His promise to return it.

How I love Him. He's ever faithful.

THE PROMISE
OF LONG LIFE

God Doesn't Lie and He Isn't Schizophrenic

Hosea 4:6
My people are destroyed for lack of knowledge....

John 8:31-32
Then said Jesus to those...who believed Him, "If ye continue in My word, you are My disciples indeed. And you shall know the truth, and the truth shall make you free."

*W*e've often heard it said that experience is the best teacher. We've also been taught that we should learn from our mistakes. These sayings are true in many ways. However, when it comes to spiritual matters, we must be wise to not solely apply natural human knowledge to gain the victory. Jesus said the Word of God is *the truth*.

It's from the Bible that we gain true knowledge. God's Word will put us in the winner's circle every time. Because we live in a world with strong influences from the evil one himself, we should be leery of believing anything that is presented to us exclusively through our natural senses—especially if it does not line up with the truths of God's Word.

Very often I speak about the mercy and goodness of God, specifically regarding physical healing. It's not possible to focus faith on the goodness of God if we base our beliefs on religious traditions or someone else's bad experiences or mistakes. When faced with a challenge such as terminal illness, we should not look at what happened to John Doe down the street. We should be asking, "What does the Bible say?" God's Word must be the final authority in every situation and circumstance.

Deuteronomy 19:15

...by the mouth of two or three witnesses the matter shall be established.

In order to have a good perspective of what God's Word says on any subject, it's best to have at least two or three scriptures to support a belief. For example, it's widely believed even by many God-fearing Christians that every person has an appointed time to die. They believe when a person's time comes, there's nothing that can be done to change it. Some may disagree, but the Bible does not teach there's an appointed time to die. There's no scriptural support for this opinion. It's true that God knows all things, and it's true He knows in advance *when* a person will die. But that does not mean it's His best if a person dies short of living a long life on the earth.

In Ecclesiastes 3:2, the Bible says there is a time to die, but it does not say there's an *appointed* time. More simply put, if Jesus tarries, everyone will face death.

Hebrews 9:27 (KJV)

*...it is appointed unto men **once** to die, but after this the judgment.*

While this passage does mention the word *appointed*, it does not reference *time*. The basic interpretation of Hebrews 9:27 is that men will die once. We are *destined* to experience physical death one time if Jesus tarries. We die and judgment follows. Man won't be reincarnated to live again in some other form nor do we get to come back as angels.

If a man or woman had an appointment with death—whether young or old—how would we explain the following scriptures?

Psalm 91:14-16

"Because he has set his love upon Me, therefore will I deliver him: I will set him on high, because he has known My name. He shall call upon Me, and I will answer him: I will be with him in trouble; I will deliver him, and honor him. **With long life will I satisfy him***, and show him My salvation."*

Proverbs 3:1-2

My son, do not forget my law, but let your heart keep my commands; **for length of days and long life, and peace they will add to you.**

Ephesians 6:1-3

Children, obey your parents in the Lord, for this is right. "Honor your father and mother;" which is the first commandment with promise: "that it may be well with you and you may **live long on the earth.***"*

God is not a man that He should lie (Numbers 23:19) nor is He schizophrenic. He doesn't say one thing but mean something else. If God intended that every person had an appointed time to die, and there was nothing anyone could do about it, why would He offer such great and wonderful promises of long life to the obedient? From the passages above, it's easy to see that long life is possible. In fact, it's not only possible, but it's also a *promise* to those who love God and obey His commandments.

Doesn't knowing about the promises of long life make it a little easier to believe that God is a good God? He doesn't want us to die prematurely or die with sickness.

It's been said, "Only the good die young." Is that true? According to Hosea 6:4, those who lack knowledge are among those who perish. The knowledge of God's Word concerning health and healing is this: God wants us to have it! That's one of the precious gifts Jesus died to provide. There are people who have been diagnosed with terminal illness who have difficulty believing God for healing because they think it might be their "time to go." They are afraid of interfering with God's will by desiring healing.

"It might be God's will for me to die now," some have said. Can you see how contrary this way of thinking is to the truth of God's Word?

"Well, if it's God's will to heal me, then He will heal me," others have said. Yet, God's Word *is* His will. God has made it clear from Genesis to Revelation that healing is a part of our covenant with Him. If someone is sick, we don't have to ask God if it's His will to heal the person. We can pray in faith, knowing He is always faithful to watch over His Word to perform it.

"What about those who die in acts of war or accidents?" someone might ask. For soldiers who have willingly taken oaths to defend their country, they have made a public declaration to lay down their lives if necessary. This is a matter of choice or will on their part. God has given each of us a free will. However, there are many wonderful promises for divine protection in the Bible. They are applicable in praying for the safety of those serving in the armed forces as well as the protection of our loved ones.

The entire 91st Psalm is an excellent example of God's promises concerning divine protection and long life. We pray and confess it regularly at our house and encourage others to do the same.

2 Corinthians 1:20
For all the promises of God in Him are Yes, and in Him Amen, to the glory of God through us.

The answer to any question concerning the will of God and his promises is, "Yes and so be it for His glory." God is not a respecter of persons (Acts 10:34). He doesn't pick favorites. If He will do it for one, He will do it for all.

Deuteronomy 29:29
The secret things belong to the LORD our God, but those things which are revealed belong to us and to our children forever, that we may do all the words of this law.

If we die prematurely, how can we continue to do "all the words of this law" in the earth? There will be times we don't understand why things happen the way they do. If God's Word is not specific on a matter or He does not personally reveal something to us, it's a "secret thing." We should simply leave it in His hands. However, the things that are *revealed* belong to us. Healing and the promise of long life have been clearly presented in His Word. Therefore, they belong to us and to our children forever.

1 John 5:14-15 (NIV)
This is the confidence we have in approaching God: that if we ask anything according to his will, he hears us. And if we know that he hears us—whatever we ask – we know that we have what we asked of him.

Ask! He will hear, and you will receive!

DEADMAN RESTORED TO HEALTH

Working with the Gifts of the Spirit in Prayer

1 Corinthians 12:1-11 (KJV)

*Now concerning spiritual gifts, brethren, I would not have you ignorant…the manifestation of the Spirit is given to EVERY MAN to profit withal. For to one… the word of wisdom, to another the word of knowledge … To another faith…the gifts of healing… the working of miracles …prophecy…discerning of spirits …divers kinds of tongues …interpretation of tongues. But all these worketh that one and the selfsame Spirit, dividing to **every man** severally as he will.*

Time and space does not permit us to discuss at length all of the operations and manifestations of the gifts of the Spirit. However, we do want to examine the fact that the gifts of the Spirit are available to every believer as the Holy Spirit wills. God desires spiritual gifts to operate in the lives of all believers, whether in a local church meeting, at the supermarket, or in prayer.

Oftentimes, we see powerful men and women of God flowing in the gifts of the Spirit effortlessly. We sometimes fail to realize the amount of time most of those ministers have spent practicing the gifts of the Spirit in prayer. For example, I have heard several ministers mention having prophesied or interpreted tongues often and at length in prayer. If the utterance gifts of the Spirit can operate in our prayer lives, then the rest of the gifts must also be available. Are we willing to pay the price to see these gifts manifest in our personal lives?

Not all believers are called to public ministry. Not all will operate in the gifts of the Spirit in church services. But all believers are called to prayer and can eventually learn to yield to the Holy Spirit in the privacy of their own homes. If we'll fill ourselves with the Word and learn to flow with the Spirit, we can accomplish glorious results for the kingdom of God. Even from a prayer closet, there's no distance or time in the realm of the spirit.

Ephesians 6:18 tells us that we should be "praying always with all prayer and supplication in the Spirit...." The phrase *in the Spirit* could be a direct reference to prayer in tongues. However, the more we study the Word and learn to work with the Spirit in prayer, the more spiritually sensitive we become. God is always looking for believers who are willing to make themselves available, yielding to Him in the spirit.

I recall one encounter early in our marriage and after Bible school that changed my whole perspective of prayer. It illustrates the gifts of the Spirit working in prayer. The story involves my cousin, Kenny, and his wife, Joan, who lived several hours away from our home in southern Indiana. They were close in age to my parents, and even though the miles separated us, my parents always made time for us to visit them regularly as I grew up.

When Kenny was 56 years old, he had a heart attack and died. He had been dead for nearly 15 minutes before anyone realized what had happened. Life-saving CPR was performed and an unsteady heartbeat restored.

At the hospital, he was placed on life-support systems, and the family was given a grim prognosis. His brain was so severely damaged that he became what the doctors termed a "thrashing vegetable."

Comatose, he was unable to sleep or eat, and his body thrashed in the bed uncontrollably. Experts said he would remain in that state until his heart gave out.

This was very disturbing to my family, especially my dad. He shared with me how he had heard Kenny in the background over the telephone. He said that Kenny moaned and groaned in such a manner that it sounded like the torments of hell.

I knew in my heart God wanted me to pray concerning this situation. However, being a young newlywed with a hectic schedule, I put it off, ignoring several strong nudges from the Lord. Honestly, my natural mind thought, *What's the use? They don't know God. How could God intervene in such a limited situation?* Finally, one evening while entertaining guests in our home, I could no longer withstand the urge to pray. I excused myself and literally *ran* to another room to pray.

As soon as my knees hit the floor, I was "in the spirit" and discerning of spirits was in operation. When I closed my eyes, I could see Kenny lying in his hospital bed more than 100 miles away. His body was overrun with demons that were biting, hitting, scratching, and clawing at him. No wonder he was thrashing in the bed! Off to one side was a putrid, grotesque figure I recognized as the spirit of death. I somehow knew that when they were finished tormenting my cousin, death planned to step in and finish him off.

Suddenly, the young woman visiting in our home was by my side praying in other tongues. Her presence gave me the courage to press forward. The next thing I knew, I was standing next to Kenny's bed. As far as I could tell, I was still kneeling in my living room, but my spirit seemed to be two places at once. The power of God was so strong that it was as though my hands would explode. I laid them on his heart and commanded it to be healed and to function normally. I did the same with his brain. The power I sensed was the gifts of healings and working of miracles operating in conjunction with the gift of special faith.

The prayer I had been putting off for days was over in a matter of a few minutes. Afterward, I related what I had seen to the young woman, and she confirmed that she had seen the same things. Then, my husband walked in and shared something truly amazing.

Bryan had not been in the room during our time of prayer, nor was he aware of our conversation or the burden I had to pray for Kenny. He explained that as soon as I left the room, a "spirit of prayer" had come upon him. He began to pray in other tongues. As he closed his eyes, he saw two women standing next to a hospital bed. The bed was covered with and surrounded by demons. As he moved in the Spirit, the demons turned their attention to him. He dealt with them, making it possible for the two women to minister to the man in the bed. Again, the discerning of spirits in operation.

The next day we received word from Joan that Kenny woke up early the next morning alert and in his right mind. In the end, the question that boggled my mind was, "Why would God go to such lengths to move in this situation?" Within a few days I visited them in the hospital and got my answer.

Two weeks prior to Kenny's heart attack, Joan had given her heart to the Lord. She had fallen so much in love with Jesus that she didn't know if her marriage could survive. In fact, her husband did not understand her new-found love and zeal for the Lord, and she asked the Lord how she could continue in her marriage. When Kenny had the heart attack, she thought God was answering her question by taking him out of her life.

On the contrary, the Word of God tells us that Jesus came to give us life abundantly (John 10:10). God is not the author of calamity or death. He wanted to make it very clear to Joan that he would not kill her husband so she could serve Him. He wanted her to know without a doubt that He was a God of love and life. Even though she was not fully aware of all the benefits of her new-found covenant, God honored His Word by healing and restoring her husband, sparing him from an eternity in hell (Acts 11:14).

Kenny came out of the hospital a few days later and began attending church with his wife. Before Joan moved to heaven, they spent 11 more years of life and love together that they would have never known had God not supernaturally intervened. Kenny passed away at the age of 85. For 29 years, the Lord used his life as a living testimony to the healing, miracle-working power that God manifested for him from within the prayer closet.

It's important to note that God did not accomplish this awesome miracle because of my faith, clearly. I was reluctant to pray and honestly didn't think that God could move through my prayers. This is why it's so important to be open to the moving of the Holy Spirit and His gifts. I was simply available, and God was looking for a willing vessel to yield to the Spirit in prayer. Even though she didn't understand, it was Joan's new-found faith that moved God. And *move*, He did. Hallelujah!

THE POWER
OF A WHISPER

*Don't Miss the Supernatural
by Looking for the Spectacular*

Romans 8:14

For as many as are led by the Spirit of God, these are sons of God.

In the Old Testament, not everyone who believed in God received the Holy Spirit. Primarily, it was the prophets, priests and kings who were anointed. Others received anointings for specific tasks, but even then, the Holy Spirit only came *upon* them.

As Jesus spoke to His disciples in John 14:17, He explained "the Spirit of truth, whom the world cannot receive...you know Him, for He dwells with you, and will be *in* you." This must have seemed like a strange idea to the disciples who were raised as Jews. They knew what it was to have the Holy Spirit *with* them. They had seen His manifestations before, but to have Him *in* them would have been an entirely different matter.

Sometimes I don't think believers today realize the importance and privilege we have in this wonderful gift of the Holy Spirit. He comes *into* us the moment we are born again. When God placed the Holy Spirit within the spirit of man at the new birth, He was doing a new thing (2 Corinthians 5:17; Isaiah 43:19). Even though we can learn from the Old Testament examples of the manifestations of God's Spirit, we cannot necessarily follow the patterns set forth there. It's only in the New Testament we see the Spirit of God actually coming into the heart or spirit of man to permanently dwell.

Often we hear believers saying things like, "Such and such happened, so I guess God wants me to do so and so...." This type of thinking is dangerous. To be led by circumstances is not God's best. Occasionally God will lead us in such a manner, especially when we're new to the things of God or just learning about following the ways of the Holy Spirit. But God's highest and best is that we're led from the inside out.

In considering these points, it's important to note that we have an "...adversary the devil..." who "...walks about like a roaring lion, seeking whom he may devour" (1 Peter 5:8). He has access to our sensory perception or can interfere with the circumstances of our lives. If we allow ourselves to be led by circumstances or the five senses, it's possible to be led astray. Whereas, if we're looking to the Holy One on the inside of us, following the inward direction He provides, we're less likely to be deceived.

Before we answer the question, "How can I be led by the Spirit of God?" let's look at a couple of Old Testament examples.

Gideon was a great man. The angel of the Lord referred to him as a "mighty man of valor." However, when the angel first approached him, he had not been anointed for service. In Judges 6:34, the Word says that the Spirit of God eventually came *upon* him, but he had no means of being led by the Spirit *within*. The anointing was for the specific task that God had placed before him. Therefore, God led Gideon through outward manifestations (Judges 6:36-40). Gideon asked God to confirm what the angel had said with a sign: dew upon a fleece of wool but not upon the ground. The next day he asked for the opposite; dew upon the ground but not upon the fleece.

Do you seek to be led by God in this manner, saying, "God, if it's really You, let such and such happen"? I hope not! Yes, it worked for Gideon, but Gideon was not born again. Gideon didn't have the Holy Spirit dwelling in his spirit. The writer of Hebrews says the new covenant is a "...better covenant, which was established upon better promises" (Hebrews 8:6). The indwelling of the Holy Spirit is one of those promises, so you and I now have better ways of being led by God.

The most common methods the Holy Spirit uses to guide a New Testament believer are the inward witness (Romans 8:16; Hebrews 10:15-17) and the inward voice, also known as the still small voice.

We get a glimpse of the still small voice in the story of Elijah. Even though Elijah was not "born again," he was anointed by the Holy Spirit as a prophet. As with many Old Testament stories, his experience is given to us as a type or shadow of what was to come in the New Testament. In 1 Kings 18, we find the awesome account of Elijah's encounter with King Ahab and the prophets of Baal. On Mount Carmel, Elijah called and God answered by fire. Afterward, Elijah slew the 400 prophets of Baal, prayed an effectual fervent prayer for rain (James 5:7-8, 16-18), and then outran the chariot of Ahab nearly 40 miles. It was an eventful and spectacular day in the life of an Old Testament prophet.

First Kings chapter 19 paints a different picture. Ahab's wife, Queen Jezebel, didn't like what Elijah had done. One would think she would have been impressed with Elijah's "spirituality" and demonstration of God's power working through him. Yet, it only served to make her angry enough to call for Elijah's assassination. Note to self: not everyone will be happy with spectacular manifestations of God.

Elijah ran for his life, a journey that eventually took him across the desert to Horeb, the mountain of God. We find it described in the following verses:

1 Kings 19:9-12

And there he went into a cave, and spent the night in that place ... And behold, the Lord passed by, and a great and strong wind tore into the mountains and broke the rocks in pieces before the Lord, **but** *the Lord* **was** *not in the wind; and after the wind an earthquake,* **but** *the Lord* **was** *not in the earthquake; and after the earthquake a fire,* **but** *the Lord* **was** *not in the fire; and after the fire a still small voice.*

There, standing in the mouth of a cave, Elijah received the direction he needed that sustained him through the remainder of his time on the earth. Once he completed all the still small voice had spoken, he was taken up into heaven in a chariot of fire. Wow! Elijah knew about spectacular manifestations of God. However, when God wanted to direct him, it was in the still small voice he found the guidance he needed.

How often do we look for the spectacular only to miss the supernatural leading of the Holy Spirit? I have a dear friend who has passionately pursued a close relationship with the Lord. She's worked diligently to develop her spiritual ears and learn to follow the Holy Spirit. One night she was awakened hearing these words: "You need to begin praying for those in your family who will preach the end-time message."

At first, she didn't understand, saying, "What, Lord?" The message was repeated, but she was so sleepy she could hardly comprehend. The same still small voice said, "Write it down." So, in the darkness she scribbled His words on paper. When she awoke the next morning, what had happened seemed like a dream. However, she found the note she had written, and it all came back to her and more. She got so excited. She knew that if she had not been listening, she would have missed it or dismissed it. The instruction she received was an important prayer assignment she will more than likely pray about the rest of her days.

Proverbs 20:27 says, "The spirit of man is the candle of the LORD, searching all the inward parts of the belly" (KJV). If a person is a believer, the Holy Spirit takes up residence in his or her human spirit. There's something to be said about going with your "gut" feeling. According to the Scriptures, the spirit is located in our innermost belly.

One minister likens the inward witness to a traffic light. He'll present a question to the Lord, and if he gets a "red light" (a scratchy, uncomfortable feeling on the inside) he stops right there. He takes that as a *no*. However, if he presents a question to the Lord, and he gets a "green light" (a smooth, velvety feeling on the inside) he will proceed.

You might ask, "How can I know this inward witness and still small voice?" Jesus said on numerous occasions in the book of Revelation, "He who has ears to hear, let him hear what the Spirit is saying...." God will talk to us. He wants us to know Him and His plans. However, it takes practice and time to develop our spiritual ears.

Prayer is a vital key to living an abundant Christian life. Prayer is not supposed to be a one-sided conversation where we talk, and He listens. It's also supposed to be that He talks, and *we listen*. The more we practice listening to the Lord in prayer, the easier it is to be led by His Spirit in our everyday lives. Another key to being led by the Spirit is to make sure we renew our minds to the Word of God. The Lord reveals Himself to us through His Word, and the more we know His Word, the more we know of Him and the more His thoughts become our own.

Let's not miss the supernatural leading of God by looking for the spectacular. Whispers can be as powerful and revealing as fire from heaven when they come from the Holy One on the inside.

PROBLEM DWARFED BY MAGNIFYING GOD

A Bigger God – An Effective Tool in Prayer

A friend in the ministry once shared about a conversation he had with a great woman of prayer. She had been involved in the early days of the Pentecostal movement in America when some say it was easier to get prayers answered. This minister asked her, "What's the difference between the way we pray now and the way you prayed back then"? Her reply was simple and direct: "That's easy. When you folks get together, you spend all your time talking about how big the problems are. When we got together, we spent all our time talking about how big God is."

Psalm 34:1-4

I will bless the LORD at all times; His praise shall continually be in my mouth. My soul shall make her boast in the LORD; the humble shall hear of it and be glad. Oh, magnify the LORD with me, and let us exalt His name together. I sought the LORD, and He heard me, and delivered me from all my fears.

Several years ago, in the early years of our marriage (when money was *tight*), I remember getting up one night worrying over finances. At the time, I was just a few weeks short of giving birth to our first child and extremely *hormonal.* I waddled the floor, stewed, and fretted, and fretted and stewed and waddled some more. Quite unexpectedly, I found myself thinking, *This is ridiculous! God has always taken care of us.*

There's not really anything I can do, and I'm not really helping by fretting. I'll just take a moment to praise the Lord to show Him I trust Him.

Sobbing and in the most pitiful voice imaginable, I bawled through a red face streaked with tears, "I praaaaise You, God. (Sniff, sniff). I looooove You, Jeeesus. I magggggnify Yooooouuuu. I maggnify Yoouu. I magnify You."

Suddenly, I found myself trying to picture what it would be like to look at God through a magnifying glass. You know, He's a pretty big God. But when we look at Him in that manner, He gets really BIG. The longer I *magnified* Him, the bigger He got. By the time I came to myself, my problems seemed like teeny tiny specks compared to the greatness of His love.

I didn't *feel* like praising Him when I began. I wanted to crawl under a rock somewhere and have a *pity party*. Praising Him was a choice I made, and He blessed me because of it. Before I knew what happened, I found myself *rejoicing* all over the living room. I went back to bed and slept in sweet peace, never fussing about that situation again. Our finances didn't turn around instantly. It took some time, but we didn't go under either.

Ephesians 5:18-20 (KJV)
...be filled with the Spirit, speaking to yourselves in psalms and hymns and spiritual songs, singing and making melody in your heart to the Lord; Giving thanks always for all things unto God and the Father in the name of our Lord Jesus Christ.

The example of magnifying God is also a good illustration of Ephesians 5:18-20. I spoke to myself. I sang and praised Him. I thanked Him. Because I did those things, He filled me up. When I poured my heart out to Him, He poured Himself into me. His joy sustained me because I chose to praise Him in that hour of darkness. He sustained me!

Nehemiah 8:10

...the joy of the LORD is your strength.

The joy of the Lord truly became my strength. Magnifying God is an awesome tool we can use in our prayer lives. How many times are we given prayer requests that seem beyond our own ability to pray through? How many times do we question whether or not we're really getting anywhere because the problems seem so big? The longer I serve Him the more desperate prayer requests seem to become. If I don't keep my focus on the Lord, the weight of those problems could become too much for me. But God's arm is never too short. According to Ephesians 3:20, "He is able to do exceeding abundantly above all that we ask or think, according to the power that worketh in us" (KJV).

Of course, the ultimate source of the *power* in our lives is the Holy Spirit, but God has given us many powerful tools to use such as His name, His blood, His Word, and *praise*. Psalm 22:3 tells us that God inhabits the praises of His people. When we praise Him, He shows up. No matter what the problem, it will melt like wax in the presence of the Lord.

Praise and thanksgiving are awesome ways to exercise or demonstrate our faith. It's not always easy to praise the Lord, especially when the challenges we face seem so great. However, it pleases the Lord when we put our fears and feelings aside to thank Him in advance. It also stays our minds, keeping them from wandering into the shadows of worry or discouragement. I can't count how many times I have gone to prayer facing insurmountable odds, only to come out with a note of victory because I magnified God.

There's an important prayer key here, and we must be certain not to miss it. David, the shepherd boy, was anointed to be King of Israel many years before he ever took his place on the throne. When did he take his rightful position? When the people of Israel *proclaimed* him king. Even though God said he was king, he did not operate in the fullness of that capacity until the people gave him that place.

We know that Jesus is King of Kings and Lord of Lords. Yet there's something to be said about *proclaiming* Him King in prayer. It reminds us of how awesome He really is—how good and how great! It also gives Him a platform from which to operate. The Holy Spirit is a gentleman, and He won't force Himself into situations. It's our responsibility to make room for the Lord, clearing the way for the King of Glory to come in.

Psalm 24:9-10
Lift up your heads, O you gates! Lift up, you everlasting doors! And the King of glory shall come in. Who is this King of glory? The LORD of hosts, He is the King of glory. Selah.

This prayer key is important when praying for nations—especially nations that may not be considered Christian. I've also seen these same principles work effectively in praying for the terminally ill. Let's face it, when we know of situations where loved ones are at death's door, those problems seem pretty big. But which is greater—cancer or God's love? Heart disease or God's mercy? Diabetes or His healing touch?

The next time we go into the prayer closet, let's make sure we're not talking about how big the problem is. Let's make sure we're talking about how BIG God is. Magnify Him! Exalt Him over *every* circumstance! By the time we get around to actually praying about *the problem*, it will be dwarfed in comparison to the greatness of our God. It's like stepping into the arena of faith behind a giant—one experienced in all types of combat and undefeated in every battle.

The Price
of Prayerlessness

We'll never know the thrill
Of seeing answers to our prayers
Never realize our full potential
Or know the peace of casting all our cares

We'll find out what it is
To barely get along
When all the while victory
Should be our only song

We can never really know
What it is that we have missed
If we never get beyond
The few family members on our list

We'll never reap the benefits
Of giving ourselves for others
Or know what is to walk in the strength
Of the prayers of our brothers

We'll only know complacency
Mediocrity is a half-hearted friend
We'll only know the ordinary
When God gives extraordinary means to an end

We'll never know what it is
To see the impossible come to pass
We'll only know the frustration of leaning to our own strength
Which never truly lasts

There is a trust; there is a confidence
That comes only from spending time with Him
Without taking time to bask in His light;
The sum of our lives grows steadily dim

So keep walking—keep talking—keep trusting
Pressing in—instead of away
Knowing the power of fellowship with the Almighty
Is a price we all should want to pay.

12/20/2005
Denise L. Shaw

WOMAN CONFESSES AND GETS LIFE

1 John 5:14-15 (NIV)

This is the confidence we have in approaching God: that if we ask anything according to his will, he hears us. And if we know that he hears us—whatever we ask—we know that we have what we asked of him.

A major key to answered prayer and living a victorious Christian life is to know the will of God. When we know the will of God, we can pray with confidence. The good news is that God's Word is His will. That means if we can find a promise in the Bible that answers our need, then we know His will concerning that situation. The more we know about the Bible, the more effective we are in prayer.

For example, God's Word is clear concerning the subject of healing. Healing is part of our redemption. Jesus paid the price for sickness when He paid the price for sin. It's amazing how often healing is mentioned in the Scriptures right along with salvation. Bottom line, healing belongs to us and for believers it is a covenant right. When we have a good understanding of this truth, we can pray in faith.

Mark 11:22-24 (NIV)

*"Have faith in God," Jesus answered. "I tell you the truth, if anyone **says** to this mountain, `Go, throw yourself into the sea,' and does not doubt in his heart but believes that what he **says** will happen,*

*it will be done for him. Therefore I tell you, whatever you **ask** for in prayer, believe that you have received it, and it will be yours."*

We've heard it said many times that "faith without works is dead" (James 2:26). "That sounds great, but what does it mean?" someone might ask. Actually, sometimes it's difficult to know how to define *works*. Salvation doesn't come to us through works; it comes by faith. There is nothing we can do to earn our salvation. It is a free gift. Healing operates the same way. We cannot *earn* our healing. It most often comes by faith. But, apparently, there's something we can *do* to activate our faith.

A key to putting our faith to "work" is found in Mark 11:22-24, which tells us that we can have what we say. There are many scriptural references to support this truth such as Romans 10:9-10 that explains our salvation comes when we believe and "confess" Jesus as Lord and Savior. We can receive healing from the Lord in the same manner—by believing and confessing.

Several years ago, I was faced with a health challenge, and I had an opportunity to put this principle to work. I had discovered a lump growing in a historically cancer-prone area for a woman. It could have been nothing since I had a past history of cysts in the same area, but it was not something that should be ignored.

I was a young mother with a busy schedule, and therefore, I didn't have time to give it much thought. I was simply aware of a potential problem. Foolishly, I didn't think it was necessary to go to the doctor. I didn't think it was life-threatening, just something I knew God could and would take care of. I decided to deal with it by faith.

So, my faith journey began. Daily for six weeks I would get up every morning and exercise my faith by speaking to my body and confessing what I believed. It went something like this: "Devil, you cannot kill me. Jesus is my Healer. His healing power is working in my body bringing about a healing and a cure. Mark 11:23 and 24 says I can have whatsoever I say, and I say that cancer can't live in my body. The healing power of God is at work in my body causing it to be healthy, whole, and well. I command every cell, every tissue, every organ in my body to function to perfection. I thank You, Lord, that You are causing me to be completely well according to Your Word. Thank You, Lord, for Your redemptive work. Thank You for healing me!"

Now, those were some pretty bold statements. Some readers may think they were too bold. However, it's what I believed (and still do), and every word was backed up in scripture. By speaking what I believed and confessing Jesus as my Healer, I was exercising my faith. However, six weeks later, nothing in my body had improved. As a matter of fact, the lump seemed to be growing.

One afternoon while walking into a prayer meeting, I casually mentioned to my husband that I might need to undergo some medical tests. I had no sense of urgency or fear. After all, I had been working the Word and peace flooded my heart.

Within the hour the situation changed drastically. As the prayer meeting was wrapping up, a minister quickly walked to the platform. Motioning with his hand to our area of the room, he said, "Someone seated in this area is having alarming symptoms of cancer. Who is it? The Lord wants to minister to you."

I sat there looking around, thinking, *Gee, I wonder who that is?* Never once did I consider he could have been talking about me. I was resting in faith because I knew the Word of God was already at work on my behalf.

Suddenly, the Holy Spirit said on the inside of me, "That's you!" Surprised, I jumped to my feet, saying, "That's me? That's me!" Before

I knew what happened, the minister had laid his hands upon me, and every symptom in my body instantly disappeared by the power of God. Moments later in a private room, I examined myself to find everything completely normal—no trace of any lump.

The growth that God removed from my body had been the size of a golf ball! A few weeks later I underwent medical testing, and the doctor confirmed there had been a large mass. He said a "void" place in the tissue where the lump had been showed up on the X-rays. It had been supernaturally removed by the mercy of God, and I had the medically documented X-rays to prove it! God is good. God is faithful. And if He'll do it for me, He'll do it for you!

As a sidenote, it's important to understand that it's possible to exercise faith while also receiving medical care. At the time, I chose to do without medical attention because I didn't understand the seriousness of my situation. However, if I had it to do over, I would have gone to the doctor much sooner. Generally speaking, in life-threatening situations, it's wise to seek the assistance of a medical professional while actively exercising your faith as well.

Proverbs 4:20-22
*My son, give attention to **my words;** incline your ear to my sayings. Do not let them depart from your eyes; keep them in the midst of your heart. For they are **life** to those who find them, and **health** to all their flesh.*

By believing and confessing the Word of God, we're able to be partakers of the abundant life Jesus died to provide. Confession is an easy and effective tool that can change the circumstances around us, forcing them to line up with the promises of God's Word. These truths not only apply to healing, but also to all the other benefits of our covenant including divine provision and protection.

John 10:10

The thief does not come except to steal, and to kill, and to destroy. I have come that they might have LIFE, and that they may have it more abundantly.

GRANNY'S LITTLE CHICKS

A Highway in the Desert—
Prepare Ye the Way of the Lord

*I*n January of 1997, the Lord began to deal with us to move to Branson, Missouri. At that same time, He directed me to an interesting passage in Isaiah 40. When I began studying it, I had little understanding of what the Lord was saying. The next few years proved to be an interesting journey as He gradually unfolded truths I'm about to share.

Let's begin with an important scripture in Isaiah.

Isaiah 40:3-5 (KJV)
The voice of him that crieth in the wilderness, Prepare ye the way of the Lord, make straight in the desert a highway for our God. Every valley shall be exalted, and every mountain and hill shall be made low: and the crooked shall be made straight, and the rough places plain: And the glory of the Lord shall be revealed, and all flesh shall see it together: for the mouth of the Lord hath spoken it.

This passage is a prophetic foretelling of John the Baptist, a cousin to Jesus sent before Him to prepare people for the first coming of the Lord. Studying his life is important as the Church is in a position now where we also prepare the world for Jesus' coming. Careful study of the Bible shows we're approaching the imminent return of Jesus to the earth—an event the Bible refers to as the Second Coming of Christ.

While the Church is still in the earth before the Rapture, it's vitally important we do our part to prepare the world—and ourselves—for His soon return.

A couple of years later, I was awakened in the night by the Lord saying, *"I've given you a voice."* Several interpretations came to mind, so I went to the Bible to make sure I was hearing from Him. As I studied, I found myself back in Isaiah chapter 40, "The *voice* of him that crieth in the wilderness…. Make straight in the desert a highway for our God…." During the time that we lived in Branson, we had opportunity to gain additional insight into this passage by witnessing an interesting construction project. Centrally located in the heart of the Ozark Mountains, Branson, Missouri, is somewhat remote, making travel difficult. Near the turn of the century, the State of Missouri created a *highway* to streamline traffic to and from Branson. Literally, valleys were exalted (raised up) and mountains made low (brought down). Crooked places were made straight and rough places plain. The highway was made smooth and clear for travelers to visit Branson with ease.

Before we discuss John the Baptist's message and what he did to make crooked places straight and rough places smooth, let's consider the meaning of a few words. First of all, the word *wilderness* in the Bible is often defined as *desert,* indicative of a dry, barren place. Western minds often think of *wilderness* as a heavily wooded area with lots of vegetation and difficult terrain. But the Bible is an Eastern book, where *wilderness* commonly refers to a sometimes mountainous desert wasteland.

Secondly, let's look at Ezekiel 47, which is a prophetic picture of the millennial Jerusalem yet to come but also symbolic of the Church in this hour. This passage describes the waters that are symbolic of the Holy Spirit that pour from the Throne of God and flow eastward toward the desert. In recent years, much of the body of Christ has experienced the beginnings of an outpouring of the Holy Spirit reviving and refreshing portions of the Church.

Notice now verses 8 and 9: "These waters…go down into the desert and go into the sea…and there shall be a very great multitude of fish… and everything shall live whither the river cometh" (KJV). For years much of the Church, especially in the United States, has been a dry and barren place—a wilderness so-to-speak. The outpouring of the Holy Spirit had to come to the Church (the desert) before it could go to the world (the sea). Jesus said He would make us fishers of men, and the outpouring of the Spirit prepares the Church to be the soul-winners Jesus said we would be. There is yet to come "a great multitude of fish" to be born into the kingdom of God, and we're on the verge of seeing it come to pass.

So what was John the Baptist's role before the coming of Christ, and what can we learn from it? John's main message was "Repent! The kingdom of heaven is at hand." Acts 3:19-20 says to the early church, "Repent ye therefore, and be converted, that your sins may be blotted out, when the times of refreshing shall come from the presence of the Lord. And he shall send Jesus Christ which before was preached unto you." We also have seen the refreshing of the Holy Spirit poured out upon the Church, and we should have been drawn into repentance and holiness. Sadly, many of those blessed by the outpouring of the Spirit got so caught up in the move of God they forgot who blessed them and missed the purpose of His move.

When I was a little girl, my grandmother often told me a story about some baby chickens she was raising in the summer of 1936. That summer was one of the hottest on record. It was very dry that year, seeing little or no rain all season. One hot July day Grandma had her little chicks in the barnyard. Unexpectedly, a heavy rainstorm blew across the hills of southern Indiana. She knew it was important to get those baby chicks out of the rain, so she rushed to bring them in. A sudden downpour began, and she and the chicks were caught in the barnyard. Since these babies had never seen rain before, they tipped their little heads upward to see what it was. In doing so, the water rushed into their noses and more than half of them drowned before she could get them to safety.

It seems this is what has happened in many churches. They got caught up in the outpouring of the Holy Spirit and nearly drowned in the blessing! So many did not reach the destination the Lord had for them—to be holy vessels He could use. ***Repent!***

Other aspects of John's ministry can be found in Luke 1:17 where the angel Gabriel described John's destiny: "And he [John] shall go before him [the Lord Jesus] in the spirit and power of Elijah, to turn the hearts of the fathers to the children, and the disobedient to the wisdom of the just; to make ready a people prepared for the Lord."

We're seeing a need for these same things in this late hour. There must have been a need for the rebuilding of families in John's day. Otherwise, it would not have been part of his commission from God. How much more is it needed today?

How many churches and ministries has God raised up in recent years to focus on the rebuilding of the family? This is a scriptural precedent for preparing the way of the Lord. If a ministry wants to express God's heart in this end time, it should have a strong emphasis on family, youth, and children.

John's mission was to make ready a people prepared for the Lord, and this is much of the mission of the Church today. There is a great ingathering of souls that must come before we leave this earth, and we must use our voices to restore families and gather in the lost.

WOMAN LAUGHS DURING SURGERY

A Merry Heart Does Good Like Medicine

1 Corinthians 1:27 (KJV)
But God hath chosen the foolish things of this world to confound the wise....

Proverbs 17:22
A merry heart does good, like medicine....

During the summer of 1992, I had the privilege of becoming acquainted with a young woman suffering a serious ailment. I'm not a doctor and wouldn't attempt to give the specifics of her condition, but I will explain that tests showed the only way to repair the problem was a dangerous and expensive operation. Apparently, there was some sort of deformity in the blood vessels of her brain that caused bizarre symptoms, including extreme nausea and dizziness. She had lost a lot of weight and suffered severe headaches.

The illness attacked her while she was a Bible school student. During this time, she became well acquainted with the biblical truths of divine health and grew more and more determined to receive complete restoration from the Lord.

Extensive medical testing had left her with imposing medical bills, far beyond her means to pay. The last thing she wanted was to undergo costly, neurological/vascular surgery. Amazingly, her faith was persistent even though the symptoms grew worse. She refused to give up!

We eventually became co-workers at a ministry in Oklahoma. In July of that year, we were assigned to help with registration at a convention downtown. Our job duties positioned us right next to each other, giving us a brief opportunity to become better acquainted.

On Tuesday afternoon during a lull in activity, she boldly said to me, "I'm going to receive the manifestation of my healing *this week*." As those words came from her mouth, something strange happened inside of me. Back then, I didn't really understand such things, but I now know it was a manifestation of special faith (1 Corinthians 12:9). Before I knew what I was saying, I proclaimed, "I'll just agree with you for that!" We then prayed a simple prayer of agreement (Matthew 18:19) and continued with our responsibilities.

Later toward the end of our shift, we had another occasion to talk and casually delighted ourselves in the goodness of God. The more we talked about Him, His goodness, His faithfulness and His Word, the more the atmosphere became charged with faith, expectancy, and joy. Suddenly, it seemed everything we said was funny, and we were beside ourselves with laughter, practically falling out of our chairs. Actually, I think we did once or twice!

We made utter spectacles of ourselves! To avoid further embarrassment and regain composure, we finally hid behind a nearby curtain. Unfortunately, the curtain we chose just happened to be the "lost and found" booth. The fact that we were hiding in "lost and found" just escalated the fiasco. Thankfully, our shift ended, releasing us from our job duties.

Eventually, I recovered, but my friend grew increasingly "lost" in exuberant joy. Because of her weakened physical condition, well-meaning friends had to help her. They dragged her down the main hallway to a booth in the exhibit hall. Not knowing what else to do, they laid her on a sofa and left her there. Her booming chuckles echoed loudly over the large hall. Many found themselves caught up in overwhelming joy because the laughter was so contagious. She continued laughing exuberantly for almost three hours. And when she came to herself, she was completely healed!

Later, I asked her to tell me from her perspective what happened that afternoon. She said as she lay on the sofa, her primary focus was on the Lord and she knew in her heart her healing was complete. This blessed her to the point of being "tickled!" (Sometimes, just like a natural father likes to tickle his own child, God likes to "tickle" us.) Somewhere in the midst of her joy, she realized that God was "operating" on her brain. She could see His hand upon her, working in intricate detail to untwist the mangled blood vessels, draining the large pocket of blood that had been adding to her symptoms daily. This blessed her all the more, keeping her in a state of exceedingly great joy for several hours.

God's method for delivering this woman is explained well by an illustration I have mentioned before concerning joy and laughter. I previously explained how a dentist oftentimes uses gas to anesthetize a patient before pulling a tooth. The gas causes the sufferer to become "intoxicated" to the point of being *happy*. The dentist can then do whatever is needed; it's painless to the patient. In the same way, God uses joy or laughter to transform His children. As they become overjoyed with His goodness and love, He can fix whatever is broken in their lives.

Amazingly, my friend's story doesn't end here. A few weeks after this precious young woman received her healing, we witnessed her in another laughing binge. This time it had to do with finances. God had instructed her to call the hospital to check on her account, which she knew to be several thousand dollars in arrears. Yet when she called, she found that the bill had been mysteriously paid in full. Her reply to the clerk was, "Oh, my Father must have taken care of it!" That is, her heavenly Father took care of it! Therefore, not only had she been healed, she had been made whole—nothing missing, nothing broken!

Even though God's ways are unique to us, He's on our side. He hears our prayers, sees our needs, and goes to work on our behalf. If we'll believe Him without wavering, He'll hasten to watch over His Word to perform it (Jeremiah 1:12).

I rejoice just thinking about it! God really does use the foolish things of this world to confound the wisdom of men.

VALIANT FARMER HIDES OUT

Leads Others in Victorious Revolt

The story of Gideon is one of the most intriguing and inspiring passages of scripture in the Old Testament, and its truths will help us as believers to become more skilled at possessing what rightfully belongs to us. Rather than listing the entire passage here, let me encourage you to follow along, beginning in Judges 6.

Midianite oppressors had held the children of Israel captive for seven years. They were forced to hide in mountains and caves, living in abject poverty. Their captivity was especially cruel because the Midianites waited until the Israelites had done all the work of planting and cultivating their crops and then destroyed or stole their harvest. Just as the harvest was ready to be reaped, the Midianites overtook them and left them without even the basics for survival.

According to Judges 6:4, the enemy took all their substance—including sheep, oxen, and donkeys. Without sheep, the Israelites had no means by which to draw near to God in worship; these animals were used to approach God through sacrifices and offerings. When the Midianites stole the oxen, they also stole their very livelihood. The oxen were tools Israel used to plant and cultivate their crops, and without these vital animals, they could not support themselves. Finally, the enemy took their donkeys, which was the main mode of transportation in Gideon's day. Without donkeys, Israel had no way to travel or escape. They were trapped, completely left to the mercy of their captors. Eventually, the situation became so dire that Israel began to cry out for help. God's response was to call upon a man of uncommon valor and wisdom—a man known in the Scriptures as Gideon.

Gideon's first appearance in the narrative is found in Judges 6:11—threshing wheat in a winepress and hiding from his oppressors. Gideon gets a lot of "bad press" about this little incident, being labeled a coward by many Bible scholars. However, the scripture does not say Gideon was a coward. Actually, threshing wheat in a winepress to deceive his enemy might be the actions of a very wise man. In fact, the angel of the Lord calls him a mighty man of valor in verse 12. For whatever reason, it was enough to get the attention of Almighty God.

It's true that Gideon doubted that God wanted to use a man such as him. However, God confirmed to him that he was the man for the job—the job of setting Israel free from its oppressors. Their enemies were great in number, and it would take nothing short of a miracle to put together an army powerful enough to defeat them. As the story unfolds, God directs Gideon to limit his army to just 300 men of uncommon courage.

Judges 7:2, 7
And the LORD said to Gideon, "The people who are with you are too many for Me to give the Midianites into their hands, lest Israel claim glory for itself against Me, saying, 'My own hand has saved me.' … Then the LORD said to Gideon, "By the three hundred men… I will save you, and deliver the Midianites into your hand…."'

There were 300 men against Midianites too numerous to count, but God loves odds like that! Divided into three companies of 100 each in the dark, each man went to his post with nothing more than a trumpet and a torch hidden in a clay jar. They did have swords, but with their hands full, they had no way to draw them (Judges 7:16). As the three companies surrounded the enemy, each man in each company blew his trumpet and broke his jar at an appointed time, igniting explosions of light all around the enemy camp. The enemies were thrown into such confusion they turned on each other and fled. Only after their enemies were on the run, did Israel draw their swords in pursuit, bringing utter defeat to the thieves of their harvest.

Let's consider their weapons in more detail:

- **A trumpet** or more than likely a shofar or a ram's horn often used as an instrument of worship. According to Psalm 22:3, God inhabits the praises of His people. To blow a trumpet in praise was often used to proclaim or welcome the manifested presence of God. It was the sound of victory! To blow a trumpet in battle was to signal the troops. Imagine the confusion 300 trumpets must have brought to the enemy's camp. They surely thought they were surrounded by an innumerable company. And, oh the victory that came to Gideon's army that night! It truly was the sound of victory!

- **A torch** within a clay pot, which was to be broken later. Proverbs 20:27 tells us, "The spirit of man is the candle of the LORD…" (KJV). This weapon most vividly points to our day when the spirit of God would dwell in the hearts of believers who would be vessels broken before the master, allowing the light of the gospel to pour forth from their hearts.

- **A sword** representative of the Word of God (Ephesians 6:17) or the offensive weapon used to seal the deal and bring complete destruction to the enemy's camp.

How can we apply the truths of this passage to our lives today? Perhaps some of us are in need of financial provision. We have faithfully sown, but not seen the harvest come into our barns. Perhaps we've even been faithful to tithe and give offerings, but when provision comes, it seems stolen by an unseen enemy. Some of us may need healing. And some of us may feel trapped with no means of escape.

Are you crying out to God for some relief?

Regardless of the circumstances, there's good news! We don't have to put up with harvest-stealers any more. If we follow the patterns set forth in the story of Gideon, we'll see victory where there's been defeat. Let us not give in to fear! Let us be men and women of uncommon valor.

We must use wisdom. It's not always necessary to proclaim to the world that we've got a crop in the field. Sometimes it's wisdom to keep quiet until we're certain the harvest is safe to protect it from those who would attempt to steal it from our grasp. The fact that Gideon was threshing in the winepress is a beautiful picture of keeping our harvest under the blood of Christ. We also should make certain we give all the glory to God. It should never be a matter of, "I won this victory with *my faith*." It's God who gives us faith, and it's God who instituted the laws of sowing and reaping in the first place. He deserves all the glory and praise.

Praise also is a vital weapon that exercises our faith and keeps our enemy in confusion. When things are rough and it looks like we might never reap the crop we've sown, keep the enemy guessing. Nothing is more confusing to him than when we praise the Lord in the midst of difficult times. Our job is to thank God in advance—before the harvest ever comes into the barn. Let us remember to shout with a voice of triumph because the victory has already been won.

It's also important to remain "broken" before the Lord. By that I mean, we put our plans aside, ever seeking to fulfill God's plan for our lives. We must keep our flesh in check, not allowing it to dominate or overshadow the light hidden in our hearts. As we make sure to line up our will with God's, He will cause His light to shine forth so brightly the enemy is blinded in his efforts to hinder or steal our harvest.

Finally, as we implement the above principles, it might not even be necessary to draw our swords. Keeping fear and flesh in check, praising the Lord regardless of what we see, and choosing to give God glory may be enough to put the enemy on the run. But isn't it good to know we have offensive weapons capable of bringing total destruction to the enemy's plans?

2 Corinthians 1:20-21 (NIV)

For no matter how many promises God has made, they are "Yes" in Christ. And so through him the "Amen" is spoken by us to the glory of God.

God's promises to us are yes and amen. When we put God's Word in our mouths, proclaiming His promises and laying hold of them with our hearts, it will cause the enemy to flee and open the door for the harvest. It's important to the Lord that believers are not hindered in their reaping. He wants us to prosper for the sake of the gospel. He wants us physically well so we can go into the entire world, allowing the light of the gospel to shine forth to a lost and dying world.

Say this with me: I will not let the enemy steal my harvest anymore. I will guard it and go after him. He has no right to it. I planted it, and I have a right to reap it!

HOME PROVIDED FOR YOUNG FAMILY

By the Goodness and Mercy of God

Psalm 23:1, 6

The LORD is my shepherd; I shall not want…Surely goodness and mercy shall follow me all the days of my life….

*L*et's look at some Bible definitions from the Strong's Exhaustive Concordance to help us better understand the above passage.

- *WANT – to lack, to be without, to have a need.*

- *GOODNESS – joyful, kind, loving, wealth, welfare, prosperity, happiness, good things (collective), gracious, moral good, bounty.*

- *MERCY – kindness, favor, and compassion*

Also, according to Webster's Dictionary, the word *mercy* has the following meanings: *"the power to forgive, refraining from harming, a disposition to be kind, blessing."*

According to Vine's Expository Dictionary of New Testament Words, *mercy* is *"God's attitude toward those who are in distress."* I have a friend in the ministry who sums up the definition of mercy as *"being treated better than one deserves to be treated."*

As the body of Christ, we've heard a lot of teaching about the goodness of God, but in studying this subject for myself, I was surprised to find the goodness of God so closely intertwined with material provision and wealth. In meditating upon these truths, the Lord reminded me of this illustration.

In the early years of our marriage, my husband and I like many young couples struggled to make ends meet. Because we lacked wisdom and experience, we made mistakes that cost us dearly. There were several lean years, but God was faithful. We were always able to pay our bills on time. God was patient and gently dealt with us on the sacrifices needed to get on top of the situation. We knew if we did our part, He'd come through for us. And He did, time and time again.

One of the major changes we made was with our housing. We had been renting a nice duplex, but it was really beyond our means to pay. We finally found a much smaller apartment (aka "the dungeon") that we could afford. With both of us working and Bryan working an extra job, we slowly began to increase our giving into the kingdom of God. We knew that was a key to getting out of debt.

Shortly before we moved from our nice duplex, I was talking with an acquaintance on the telephone and told her we were moving and if they ever decided to leave the area, we liked their house. We had only seen it once briefly, but I liked the blue color and thought it would be a nice place to rent.

Nevertheless, we moved the end of May into our dingy, little apartment. It was a rough time, but somehow the Lord began to dig us out of the hole we had made for ourselves. In my heart I longed for a home. Every time I'd think about a home, I'd think about the house our friends owned. If I had a dream home, that would have been it. I began to see us moving and then I'd picture in my mind that pretty blue house. Not that I really had to have *that particular* house, but it was a way for me to focus my faith.

The following January we received a call from the owner of the blue house asking if we'd like to buy their home. They were moving and remembered my comment about liking their house. I was shocked! I explained that we loved their home, but we certainly were not in a position to *buy* a home. She said, "Why don't you contact a mortgage company and see how much money you would qualify to borrow?" I consequently found that we didn't qualify for anything! Even though we had an excellent credit rating, our outgo was more than our income. It just couldn't be done. I tried explaining this to her, but she insisted there had to be a way.

They invited us once again to their home. It was much bigger and newer than I had remembered; it was less than two years old. When we left, they encouraged us to contact a mortgage company again and find out just what it would take for us to qualify for a loan. We found out we needed several thousand dollars to pay down some of our debt.

In the meantime, the owners offered us a deal we could hardly refuse—a purchase price 50% below the market value of the home. However, when we added up all the figures, we discovered that our monthly payment would still be too high, and we would have to sacrifice some of our giving. We knew we couldn't afford to give up on the plan the Lord had given us, so we declined their offer. Ouch! That was hard.

Five minutes later, we received another call from the owners. They had decided to come down even more to 40% of the market value. They said that God told them that it was our house, and they were to do whatever it took to see that we got it. Within a couple of weeks, the Lord supernaturally provided an anonymous gift, putting us in a position to qualify for the mortgage.

We moved the end of May, one year after moving into "the dungeon." The house was decorated in my taste with colors I had selected for our home when Bryan and I had first gotten married. We didn't have to change one single thing. It was perfect! Our monthly house payment was less than what we had been paying in rent for the apartment. Our car was paid off, along with many of our other bills. God had done exceeding abundantly above all we could ask or think (Ephesians 3:20).

Right before we took possession of the home, the woman called me aside and said, "Denise, I have to share something with you. The Lord wants me to tell you that your faith didn't get you this house. He is giving you this house because of His love, His goodness, and His mercy."

That was hard to take at the time, because it seemed as though our faith had won a major victory. Yet, in reality, believers often fail to give God the credit when He shows off. He's the One who gives us faith, and our faith increases as we increase in the knowledge of His Word. But it was God who gave us His Word. It is God who is merciful and kind, and it is God who treats us better than we deserve to be treated.

What a faithful, loving, and *good* God we serve. Thank God for His *mercy!*

The awesome thing to remember is that God is no respecter of persons (Acts 10:34). If God did it for us, He's more than willing to do it for you!

SOME ASSEMBLY REQUIRED

Pay Close Attention to the Instructions

The holidays often bring fond memories especially to parents. They remember their children's first Christmas—her first baby doll, his first train set. Then there's the ever- memorable assembly of a child's first bicycle. Some parents purchase the gift pre-assembled from the store but for most families the task is left for Dad or Mom on Christmas Eve.

It's truly amazing how something so big could come in such a small box with all those little pieces and parts. "Are you sure we need all these screws?" says mother. "I know how to do it," says Dad as the instructions are tossed to the side. The bicycle has been purchased and all the parts are there in one location, but it's not really a bicycle until it's fully assembled.

In the same way, there is a big difference between being gathered in one place in a church building and being assembled as a body of believers.

Hebrews 10:25 (AMPC)
Not forsaking or neglecting to assemble together [as believers], as is the habit of some people, but admonishing (warning, urging, and encouraging) one another, and all the more faithfully as you see the day approaching.

From the original Greek, the word translated *assemble* means *a complete collection*. Common meanings in the English language are *to bring, pull or come together; put or fit together, build, compile, connect, or construct*. The assembling of the church is not supposed to be a mere gathering. The apostle Paul said in 1 Corinthians 12:12, "For as the body is one and has many members, but all the members of that one body, being many, are one body, so also is Christ" (NKJV).

A bicycle has many parts; separately they are simply screws, handlebars, tires, pedals, and gears. But, collectively assembled according to the instructions, they become one bicycle. Each part may have its own identity but without the other pieces some are utterly useless. What good is a pedal if there is nothing for it to propel?

1 Corinthians 12:17
If the whole body were an eye, where would be the hearing? If the whole were hearing, where would be the smelling?

The little streamers often found flowing from the handlebars on a little girl's bike are lovely. However, if they were the only part, there'd be no way of transporting the child from point A to point B. She'd have nowhere to sit.

1 Corinthians 12:19
And if they were all one member, where would the body be?

We wouldn't have a bicycle; we would have pom-poms.

Twice in the New Testament, the apostle Paul uses the Greek word *epichoregia*, which is translated as *supply or supplies*. We see it in Philippians 1:19 regarding prayer and "...the supply of the Spirit..." and again in Ephesians 4:16 "...from whom the whole body, joined and knit together by what every joint supplies, according to the effective working by which every part does its share, causes growth of the body for the edifying of itself in love."

The parts of a bicycle must be jointed together in order for it to function as the manufacturer intended. Every piece has a part to play. For example, it's nearly impossible to ride a bike with only one pedal or without a chain to help turn the gears.

So it is with the church. Every believer has a part to fulfill within the local congregation and the body of Christ as a whole. Every believer has a supply to make. We are first gathered together, and then we are assembled. Someone might say, "I can't do anything. I'm just a babe in the Lord."

But are you hungry for more of God? Do you desire to know more of His Word? Do you long to worship Him? Then you have a supply to make!

Some believers don't realize the importance of sincere, heart-felt worship. It improves the function of the local church from the least to the greatest, and it's a supply anyone can make. Worship brings with it the presence of the Lord, which in turn provides blessing for the entire congregation.

It's also such a blessing to have those in the flock who are hungry for the Word of God. When Bryan and I pastored, we had a new believer in our church so hungry for God we found her sitting on the front row nearly every Sunday. Her desire literally drew things out by the Holy Spirit. That kind of hunger makes the speaker a better preacher. Her spiritual hunger was the supply she made, and the whole congregation benefited. It's the same in the physical realm when a growling tummy insists the whole body heed its message of hunger.

Of course, there are many different positions believers can fill in the local church. Where would we be without ushers and greeters, parking lot attendants, nursery workers, people of prayer, or teachers? There is something for everyone. According to Ephesians 4:16, once every part makes its supply it brings growth to the body. Some believers become frustrated if their church is not growing. There are lots of reasons why these things happen. But, first and foremost, we should examine ourselves to see if we're merely gathering or allowing ourselves to be assembled. Is each one doing his or her part?

Over the many years we've been involved in ministry, it has always disturbed me to hear folks say they don't have a need to go to church, saying they can get fed by watching Brother So-and-So on television. Don't misunderstand me. Christian television is a wonderful thing, but God never intended for it to replace the local church. Yes, it's true we can be spiritually fed through books, MP3s, videos, television, and even the Internet. But where is the spiritual supply? Church is not just about receiving. Where is the giving of ourselves as unto the Lord? For the body of Christ to function as God intended, we must assemble according to God's instructions found in His Word.

Some local churches are not "bicycles," so to speak. Some are gigantic machines sent forth to bring in the harvest. It's a thrill to see a combine, a farm implement used in harvest, working in the field. However, without proper maintenance that machine would break down and cease in its purpose. The local church must be well oiled by the Holy Spirit and fueled by the Word of God in order to accomplish its task. It must have a pastor who knows how to operate it—one sensitive to its every need.

Someone might say, "But there are no good churches in my area."

My response would be, "There could be if one had you as part of the assembly."

Again, Hebrews 10:25, admonishes us, "Not forsaking the assembling of ourselves together, as the manner of some is; but exhorting one another: and so much the more, as ye see the day approaching" (KJV).

It's not just a matter of having more church services. It's a matter of each of us faithfully finding our place. The day of the Lord is nearly upon us. Let us be found well assembled and doing all to fulfill our divine destiny.

WOMAN SINGS DURING CHILDBIRTH

Child's Life Spared—
Principle of Prayer Illustrated

Micah 4:9-10

For pangs have seized you like a woman in labor... labor to bring forth, O daughter of Zion, Like a woman in birth pangs. ... the LORD will redeem you from the hand of your enemies.

Several years ago, when I was expecting our second child, I didn't want to go through another childbirth like the first experience, so I asked the Lord to help me. After much heartfelt prayer, the Lord tenderly promised this time would be different.

When our first daughter was born, we had uncertainties about the birthing process. Even though we endeavored to build our faith, fear of the unknown still tried to grip me. The night after we brought her home from the hospital, my husband and I took a long look at our experience and agreed not to have another child for a *long* time.

Yet, two years and nine months later we found ourselves preparing for another delivery. The baby was 10 days overdue, and our church was in the midst of a huge camp meeting. I went every night hoping to somehow convince the baby it was time to be delivered. Just before the service started on Friday evening, I heard the Lord say, "You must yield to the Holy Spirit. It will not be easy, but it will be good." In my natural way of thinking, I expected the Holy Spirit to instruct me to do something unusual like dance in the aisle or run around the building. In the end, nothing like that happened, and I left wondering if I had missed God.

The next morning, I woke up in labor. Bryan and I along with my mother-in-law slowly made our way to the hospital. My closest friend met us there, and we settled in for what was expected to be a smooth delivery. By mid-afternoon, the labor pains became stronger but didn't seem to be making much progress. The nurse noticed I handled the contractions better when my mouth was moving, so she kindly suggested I sing to fill the time. That was the beginning of the yielding the Lord had spoken to me about the night before.

Upon hearing her suggestion, I thought, *I just will!* For me singing came more naturally than having a baby. When the next pain began, I didn't stop to think. I just opened my mouth and sang. The song was surprisingly appropriate: "The Lord is my strength and my shield. My heart trusted in Him, and I was helped. Therefore, my heart greatly rejoices, and with my song, I'm going to praise the Lord."

From then on, I sang through contractions. Within minutes my body calmed down, and the whole atmosphere changed. The clock seemed to stand still, but at the same time, the minutes flew by. As we worshipped the Lord, the room became charged with the power of His awesome presence. The nurses marveled at the sound they heard down the hall wondering, *Was this a woman in labor?* There was no hint of strain as the melodies poured from my heart. Apparently, it was noised abroad throughout the maternity ward, which became an important factor later in the story.

Things went so well so quickly we actually had to wait a few minutes for the doctor to arrive. Once he got there, things got interesting! Just moments after I began pushing out the baby, alarms sounded in the room. The baby's heart rate quickly dropped to only a few beats per minute. She was near death. The emergency response team came in seconds.

When people in our wing of the hospital heard there was a problem, they immediately started praying. They said, *"Oh, no! Not the lady who's been singing!"* While God held the life of our precious child in the palm of His hand, complete strangers gathered outside our hospital room to pray. We found it interesting that in the midst of turmoil and confusion, the Holy Spirit had superbly gathered an army of prayer warriors to stand in the gap. Afterward, we discovered that my mother-in-law had been led to pray for our doctor to have Spirit-led wisdom. My husband was inspired to pray for the baby while my dear friend prayed for me. The Lord had seen to it that all aspects were covered in prayer.

The surgeon on call wanted to do emergency surgery, but our doctor knew there was no time. The cord was tightly wrapped around the baby's neck. The doctor urgently instructed me to change my position to ease the pressure on the cord, allowing more blood to flow to the baby's body. It worked! My child's heart rate came back up, relieving the immediate danger.

It was not possible to sing at this point because of the strain on my body, but I spoke God's Word with authority. Boldly I prayed in tongues and quoted scriptures like: "This child will live and not die" (Psalm 118:17). After my baby recovered from the incident, the doctor allowed me to push once again. He gave firm instruction that the child must come quickly, and with supernatural strength, she was out in two pushes.

The baby's limp body was blue. She was in shock! After resuscitation, they let me hold her briefly before they whisked her away to the "special care" nursery for observation. Glory to God! He is faithful!

Much to the doctors' surprise, our precious daughter and I were both ready to go home in less than 24 hours.

Sometime later my mother reminded me that both of my grandmothers had lost baby girls due to cord accidents at birth. Was it a curse? No. My covenant with God has redeemed me from such things (Galatians 3:13; Ezekiel 18:17). But if the devil gets by with something in one generation of a family, he'll probably try to do it again in future generations. He doesn't have any new tricks. Yet, because of God's faithfulness we were prepared in advance for the enemy's attack. Thank God for His Word and the blood of Jesus. By winning this victory, Satan's evil chain of destruction was broken. As we worshipped the Lord in the midst of travail, just as in Micah 4:10 the Lord truly delivered us from the hand of our enemy.

"What does this story have to do with prayer?" someone might ask. The Word of God likens intercessory prayer to the travail of childbirth. Having participated in many prayer groups for the lost and for the nations, I've often witnessed what could be termed *birthing* in prayer.

The truth is, when it comes to prayer in general, sometimes the joy of our salvation often escapes us right along with the victory. We can get so caught up in our efforts, we forget to rejoice. Some individuals even step over into the realm of "works," not allowing the Holy Spirit to effectively aid them with their petitions (2 Chronicles 20:15).

Yet, one of the easiest ways to yield to the Holy Spirit in prayer is by taking a spiritual step up, magnifying the Lord with the prayer of worship (Acts 16:25; 2 Chronicles 20:21-22). By thanking God for what He has already done, we enter the arena of faith, exalting Him as Lord over the situation. Then, even the most difficult circumstances become easy to pray through to victory.

As a point of contrast, right after our second child was born, I looked at my husband and said, "I could do this again tomorrow."

"Me, too!" he said.

That's the way prayer should be! We should be able to enter in to the realm of prayer and come out refreshed, ready to face whatever challenge comes our way.

OVERTAKEN BY A GREAT WIND?

He's Still Speaking Peace

*M*ark 4:1-20 is one of the most important passages in the New Testament. It contains the parable of the sower. We will not list the entire passage here, but let me encourage you to look at it in your Bible as you read along.

The parable of the sower, also found in Luke 8 and Matthew 13, is the essence of the kingdom of God. The parable teaches us that the Word of God is the seed, and when the seed is planted in good soil, it will produce a great harvest. It will produce the abundant life Jesus came to provide.

In examining the parable of the sower, we recognize it's the Word of God the enemy tries to steal, smother, or bring to no effect in our lives. We also recognize the Word of God and its principles are keys to successful Christian living, and the Word bearing fruit in our lives is the last thing the devil wants to see happen.

It's no coincidence that after hearing the Word through this parable, the disciples immediately faced one of the biggest faith challenges of their lives.

Mark 4:35-38

On the same day, when evening had come, He said to them, "Let us cross over to the other side." Now when they had left the multitude, they took Him along in the boat as He was. And other little boats were also with Him. And a great windstorm arose, and the waves beat into the boat, so that it was already filling. But He was in the stern, asleep on a pillow. And they awoke Him and said to Him, "Teacher, do You not care that we are perishing?"

Right now in the body of Christ, it seems there are many in that same situation. We've received the Word, and we're on the verge of seeing it produce awesome fruit in our lives and in the kingdom. Yet, it seems that the enemy is doing as much as he can to steal the seed of the Word to keep it from producing an abundant harvest in the earth.

I wonder how long it took the disciples to decide to wake the Master? How long did they try to deal with the situation with their own efforts – bailing, pitching, and rowing? The ship was ready to go under before they called upon Him for help. When they did call on Him, did they call in faith? "Don't you care we are perishing?" sounds like a blame game to me.

Mark 4:39
Then He arose and rebuked the wind, and said to the sea, "Peace, be still!" And the wind ceased and there was a great calm.

If Jesus didn't care, He would have let the ship sink. Not only did He care, but He also did something about it. Are you being tossed about by a great wind? Is your ship on the verge of sinking? The words "peace be still" are still ringing throughout the earth—eternally bringing calm and serenity to lives filled with turmoil and dismay.

John 14:27
Peace I leave with you, My peace I give to you; not as the world gives do I give to you. Let not your heart be troubled, neither let it be afraid.

Again, I had the awesome opportunity of visiting Israel several years ago, including the region of Galilee. During that time the water was never still. Mountains on three sides surround it, producing a "tempest in a teapot" effect. The climate and constantly changing weather conditions cause the lake to be continually tossed and rough. Sailing on a tour boat across the Sea of Galilee, it was easy to understand how truly miraculous it must have been when Jesus commanded it to be still. When He spoke, not only did the waters quiet down, but there was a *great* calm.

Do you need great calm in your life? Have you been overtaken by a great wind? Does it look like you're going under if something doesn't change? My friend, Jesus cares. His peace is still in the earth and is available to us when we call on Him.

What happened next in the boat with Jesus and the disciples?

Mark 4:40
But He said to them, "Why are you so fearful? How is it that you have no faith?"

Jesus rebuked them for having no faith. How did He know they had no faith? They were afraid and had no peace. They should have used their faith to keep from perishing, to refuse fear, and to make it to the other side. The scripture does not specifically say which of these Jesus referred to, but perhaps it was all of the above. He did say they were going over to the other side, didn't He? The Word of God in Psalm 91 promises divine protection and long life, and the disciples should have been well acquainted with this verse.

What about you? Is your ship ready to sink? Hasn't God's Word promised abundance and victory to you?

2 Corinthians 2:14 (KJV)
Now thanks be unto God, which always causeth us to triumph in Christ....

Was it even necessary for the disciples to wake Jesus? Could they have ridden the storm out? Would they have gone under? Could they have done something about it? The scripture does not specifically say what Jesus thought the disciples should have done, but Jesus made it clear they should have been in faith.

Today as believers living under a new and better covenant, we can have faith not to perish, and we can do something about the storms that attempt to overtake us.

Matthew 28:18-20 (KJV)
And Jesus came and spoke unto them, saying, All power is given unto me in heaven and in earth…go ye therefore…I am with you always.

Philippians 2:10-11
That at the name of Jesus every knee should bow, of those in heaven, and of those on earth, and of those under the earth, and that every tongue should confess that Jesus Christ is Lord, to the glory of God the Father.

Jesus has given us His authority and His name to accomplish His will on earth. Anytime we face obstacles that prevent us from doing what God called us to do or from living an abundant life, He's given us authority to speak to those storms for ourselves using His name. All the authority of heaven is wrapped up in His name. We have the right and privilege to speak to those things that attempt to put us under, causing them to be of no effect. He wants us to speak peace to situations filled with turmoil and fear.

Don't wait until you're on the verge of sinking to call upon the Master. Don't be moved by a great wind. Don't cower down, hoping the storm will blow over. Don't let the enemy of your soul rob you of the precious victory Jesus has already won. Let Jesus' peace rule in your heart and mind. Let faith arise in your soul, confident that God is well able to carry you over to the other side to a place of victory and quiet rest. Use the name of Jesus and speak to the wind and waves, expecting great calm and total victory.

I've said it before, and I'll say it again. Jesus is still speaking peace.

SHIPWRECK PREVENTED BY RESCUE

Fighting the Good Fight of Faith Can Get Ugly

1 Timothy 1:18-19 (AMPC)

This charge and admonition I commit in trust to you…so that you may wage the good warfare. "Holding fast to faith (the leaning of the entire human personality on God in absolute trust and confidence)…some individuals have made shipwreck of their faith.

1 Peter 5:8

Be sober, be vigilant, because your adversary the devil walks about like a roaring lion, seeking whom he may devour.

Regardless of who we are, how much of the Bible we know, or how many times a week we go to church, eventually we're certain to encounter our adversary. One of his goals is to destroy our faith, rendering us ineffective for the kingdom of God.

Paul told Timothy to "…fight the good fight of faith…" (1 Timothy 6:12). What is the good fight of faith? It's the steps we take to *stay* in faith as we face the challenges of life—steps like prayer and Bible study.

Several years ago, I faced one of the most difficult faith challenges I had ever experienced when a precious loved one was stricken with terminal cancer. I was familiar with exercising faith for myself, but exercising faith for someone else is a completely different arena. Mark

11:23-24 is an excellent example of the prayer of faith. It's a perfect scripture to use when we pray regarding our personal needs such as healing or financial provision. Properly applied, it works every time.

However, that same prayer of faith cannot always be prayed as effectively for someone else. God has created each of us with our own individual will, so when we pray for someone else, his or her spiritual condition or level of understanding can factor into the equation. In such instances, it's important to follow up with other types of prayer such as intercession or supplication in the spirit (Ephesians 6:18). This insures that all the bases are covered.

When I learned of my loved one's illness, I told her I believed that the Word of God could help her. I volunteered to do whatever it took to teach her about healing. She flatly refused even the simple offer of books or recorded lessons on the subject. "You can keep your books and tapes, but you can pray if you want to," she replied.

Her request took all the responsibility off of her, and because I loved her, placed it squarely upon my shoulders. I had my hands full considering she knew very little of the Word of God regarding healing plus she made it clear she had no intention of learning.

During the following months, I toiled many hours in prayer, but foolishly and senselessly, I got over into the area of works. In frustration, I ceased to cast my care upon the Lord. Frankly, I wasted a lot of time. As her illness progressed, so did my stress level. I would wake up in the middle of the night thinking God was waking me up to pray. I'd pray for two and three hours every night. Frankly, that was not God. It was insomnia brought on by stress. I finally started getting a clue that something wasn't right when I ended up in the hospital emergency room.

It was as if there was a storm going on in my body; stress was taking its toll. By this time, my own faith was so weak I was not able to receive healing for myself. So, the last few months of this "good fight of faith" I was faced with all sorts of medical treatments and special diets to deal with the drastic symptoms in my own body. The enemy had successfully rendered me ineffective. Foolishly, I had not stayed built up in the Word of God.

I must admit, it was one of the darkest hours of my Christian experience. I felt like such a faith failure. But all the while, the Lord was there, gently encouraging me, carrying me in His loving arms. Actually, never before had I experienced such supernatural ministry from the Holy Spirit. During those long months of prayer, He would speak to me so clearly about my loved one. He showed me things that helped me understand why her heart seemed so hardened to the truth of His Word and why she seemed determined not to be healed.

He did not answer all my questions about this situation, but He did show me enough to help me recognize it wasn't up to me or my faith for her to receive healing. It was up to her. He had given her a will of her own, and for whatever reason, her will did not match mine or God's in this juncture.

As a sidenote, we know it's God's will for all to be saved, but sadly, that doesn't mean all will be saved. Again, each individual makes his or her own choice. In the same way, even though it may be God's will to heal all, that doesn't mean all will be healed. For many different reasons, there are times healing is not received. God's best is for a believer to finish his or her course after a long life, curl up, and "fall asleep" or move to heaven without sickness as did the patriarchs of old.

By the time of my loved one's death, my faith was dangerously close to being shipwrecked. The residual effects of this long battle stayed with my body for weeks after her passing. Honestly, I began to wonder if I would ever be able to pray the prayer of faith again. I didn't doubt God or His ability to heal, but I did doubt my own ability to exercise faith. Mark 11:23-24 wasn't working for me. Something was missing. I didn't believe in myself anymore.

Then something amazing happened. Two months after my loved one entered eternity, my husband and I attended a week-long seminar. The minister conducting the meeting was widely known for a tremendous healing anointing. Over many years, he had great success with the sick healed under his ministry. On the last night of the seminar, the minister offered to pray for the sick. I thought, *Now's my opportunity!* However, before I could even get out of my seat to go to the altar for prayer, the minister said, "Before you come down for prayer, examine your heart. If you're not in faith, don't even bother to come down. You must be in faith to receive healing in this service." My heart sank. I looked down deep on the inside. At the time, I honestly didn't think I had enough faith to receive healing, even if it was through a proven minister of the gospel. I stayed in my seat.

All day long the next day, I regretted not going down the night before, thinking, *You should have let him pray for you. If you had, you wouldn't be feeling so sick right now. You would be healed.* Perhaps subconsciously, the devil wanted me to think I didn't deserve to be healed because my faith had failed and my loved one had died of that terrible illness. What a lie! The devil was the one who killed that loved one— not me. It wasn't my fault. I had gone above and beyond the call of duty. At this point, it was no longer a good fight of faith. It was ugly and getting uglier by the moment.

Finally, Sunday came and our church service that morning was unusual. The atmosphere seemed to be charged with the very presence and glory of God. By offering time, everyone seemed excited about the things of God. The choir stood up to sing a song titled *Laugh at the*

Devil, even though I must admit I didn't feel like laughing. I felt like going to the restroom and losing my breakfast.

The soloist sang, "The devil said what?" Suddenly, on the inside of me, I heard the Holy Spirit say, "You don't have any faith." It was as if He answered the song's question: "The devil has been saying to you, 'You don't have any faith.'"

At that moment, all heaven broke loose on the inside of me. Knowing that the devil is the father of lies, I finally realized I had believed a lie. If the devil tells me I don't have any faith, then the opposite must be true. "I do have faith! I do have faith!" I found myself shouting. Peals of heartfelt laughter followed. In the next instant, my pastor walked to the pulpit and said, "Someone here has been experiencing chronic stomach problems. Come down here. God wants to heal you." I was in the altar before he was even finished speaking. He laid his hands upon me, and within a very short time, I was eating pizza again.

The storm of life had battered my faith to the point of shipwreck, but just before I hit the rocks, God in His infinite mercy reached down with His loving Hand and pulled me to safety.

He rescued me! And He will do the same for you!

DEATH WHERE IS YOUR STING?

Grave, Where Is Your Victory?

The death of a loved one is never an easy thing to experience. However, we don't have to face it alone.

1 Thessalonians 4:13-14, 18
But I do not want you to be ignorant, brethren, concerning those who have fallen asleep, lest you sorrow as others who have no hope. For if we believe that Jesus died and rose again, even so God will bring with Him those who sleep in Jesus... Therefore comfort one another with these words.

Notice that the Bible refers to those who have died in the Lord as being *asleep*. The word *sleep*, in its most basic definition, means *to rest the body—a temporary state without ordinary consciousness.* Human beings are created in three parts: spirit, soul, and body. We are spirit beings. The *real* you is spirit or the part of you that is recreated when you are *born again*. The mind, will, intellect, and emotions comprise the soul and are closely intertwined with the spirit (Hebrews 4:12), almost to the point of being inseparable. The spirit and soul live in a physical, flesh and blood body. When the body dies, the spirit and soul move out of the *earthly house* to take on immortality.

Paul said in 2 Corinthians 5:8 to be absent from the body is to be present with the Lord. God does not view death as we humans do. In other words, death is not the end of existence; it's simply a transition

---

from a temporary state to an eternal one. For those who have loved ones who step over to heaven, it's important to keep an eternal perspective. First Thessalonians 4:13 tells us to "...sorrow not, even as others which have no hope." In Christ Jesus we have the promise of eternal life. Therefore, those loved ones who "fall asleep" in the Lord have simply moved from this world into eternity. We shall see them again. There is hope. That same scripture passage also says, "But I would not have you to be ignorant, brethren...."

In my own life, I've experienced the loss of a parent and grandparents. I know what it is to face grief and miss people I cherish. However, because I was not completely ignorant concerning death, I was able to keep the proper perspective and not be paralyzed with grief as some are.

1 Corinthians 15:51-52, 54-55

Behold, I tell you a mystery: We shall not all sleep, but we shall all be changed—in a moment, in the twinkling of an eye, at the last trumpet. For the trumpet will sound, and the dead will be raised incorruptible, and we shall be changed ... "Death is swallowed up in victory." "O Death, where is your sting? O Hades, where is your victory?"

A few years ago, a friend of mine was going through a difficult time. Her father had passed away quite suddenly just days before the birth of her first child. She was not able to attend his funeral because of her condition. When the time came to deliver her son, she had to have emergency surgery because the baby was in the wrong position. Not only was she facing the new challenges of motherhood, but she also had to recover from major surgery and deal with the death of her father all at the same time. We can only imagine what that must have been like. However, she kept her gaze firmly upon the One from whom help comes.

One night when it seemed the pain and disappointment were more than she could bear, the Holy Spirit brought a scripture to her. It was 1 Corinthians 15:55: "Death, where is your sting? Grave, where is your victory?" It suddenly occurred to her that her father would see her son one day and the two would get to know each other in eternity. With this perspective she was able to put aside her feelings of loss and take comfort in the fact that even in death, there's no victory for our enemy. After the Lord reminded her of that passage, she was comforted so much that her grief was short-lived. She was able to go on with her life with no long-term effects from the sudden blow the enemy had dealt to her family.

According to 1 Corinthians 15:26, death is the last enemy to be destroyed. Because of what God did for us at Christ's resurrection, death is only a temporary state for our bodies. First Corinthians 15 and 1 Thessalonians 4 make it clear that those who *sleep* in Christ Jesus shall rise to live again. Not only will they rise, but also they will have new bodies. These new bodies will no longer be laden with sickness or disease, and they will never grow old. That's something to shout about! Hallelujah!

In keeping an eternal perspective, it's important to recognize the source of death. Contrary to popular opinion and religious tradition, God is not in the business of taking people's lives. John 10:10 tells us that Jesus came to give abundant life. The thief or the devil is the one who steals, kills, and destroys. Too often God gets blamed for death and destruction when He's had absolutely nothing to do with it.

Don't get me wrong. Of course, when believers enter eternity, God gladly receives them unto Himself. But that doesn't mean it was His will for them to die at that time or in that manner. There are times when God's will is not carried forth in the earth. As we said earlier, it is

God's will for all to be saved and healed, and yet, do all receive Him as Savior and Healer? No.

We have an adversary who roams about like a roaring lion, seeking whom he may devour (1 Peter 5:8). There are all sorts of reasons why things happen the way they do, but our loving Father gets the blame far too often. It's hard to see a family lose a parent or a child. It hurts to lose a loved one. We miss them. But if we can keep our eyes on the Lord and allow Him to comfort us in sorrow, He truly can give us beauty for ashes, the oil of joy for mourning, and the garment of praise for the spirit of heaviness (Isaiah 61:3).

There are times when the love of God has been more real to me than life itself, especially during times when I've lost loved ones. He was right there with me, gently ministering, giving strength and courage when my heart grew faint. During those times, I've experienced the reality of spiritual things and understood them like never before.

I remember when a precious loved one passed away a few years ago. It had to be one of the most difficult things I had ever faced. My dear one died of skin cancer, scarred and grotesque all about her head and face. It was the most awful thing I had ever witnessed. As previously described, she did not receive healing, but it was not God's fault. He was happy to receive her unto Himself when she breathed her last breath on earth.

While in prayer shortly before this loved one moved to heaven, God gave me a vision of her being caught away into glory. Right before my eyes, the beauty of her youth was restored to her. I can't tell you what that meant to me—how beautiful it was to see such a transformation. Then, in the next instant, I caught a glimpse of the devil wearing that awful tumor on his head. I suddenly realized that's how *just* our God is. Our adversary, the perpetrator of sickness and disease, will bear the full brunt of all the suffering he has placed on humanity as part of his eternal punishment. The next time I see the devil, I thoroughly expect to see him wearing that tumor on his head!

That little mini-vision changed my whole perspective. I literally laughed out loud! God helped me exchange the ashes and mourning for beauty and the oil of joy. At this dear one's graveside service, it was such a privilege to sing with all in attendance the song, "I'll Fly Away." I could almost hear her rich alto voice joining in.

Sometimes things happen that we may not understand, but we must not blame God. We must allow the Holy Spirit, our Comforter, to minister to us in ways that only He can, driving despair away with a whisper. If we focus upon the truths of God's Word, death will have no sting; the grave will have no victory. We will be free to go on with our lives knowing that God is faithful!

THE DISTRACTED BRIDE

Never Underestimate the Power of Praying in Other Tongues

*F*rom time to time, I receive prayer assignments through dreams or night visions. They are generally for my own personal prayer projects and seldom do I share them outside the prayer closet. However, there's one assignment I feel compelled to share with others, especially people of prayer.

Let me preface this by saying God's Word is true. He is Faithful. He will receive unto Himself a glorious Church without spot or wrinkle (Ephesians 5:27). I believe the dream below gives an accurate picture of how we should pray concerning the bride of Christ or the universal body of Christ and the current condition of the Church.

Let me outline the characters in my dream as follows:

- **The Bride** – symbolizing the body of Christ or believers today

- **The Bridegroom** – symbolizing Jesus

- **The mother** – symbolizing organized religion or perhaps even old-time Pentecostals who "birthed" the church of today

- **Ministers** – as we know them to be

- **The prophet** – representing the Word of the Lord, speaking for God Himself

---

141

In my dream, the bride suddenly realizes her wedding is only 10 minutes away, and she's not ready. She frantically gathers friends to help her as she makes her way to the ceremony. All too quickly, she becomes distracted—consistently forgetting what she's doing and where she's going.

The bride arrives at the church thirty minutes late and is distraught thinking, *The groom has waited so long he must be heartbroken to think I could have forgotten!* The bride is greeted at the door by her mother and quickly whisked into a room to dress. Her mother has forgotten to bring *everything* but the dress. There are no shoes. Her undergarments are the wrong color. She is beyond frustrated and embarrassed.

Unwilling to make the groom wait any longer, the bride makes her way to the foyer. An usher offers his arm just as she notices her gown isn't fastened properly. She turns away to correct it. The usher moves away and joins a group of ministers congregated in the lobby. The ministers are distracted with deep conversations about doctrine, trying to outdo one another with testimony after testimony. They don't notice or care that *The Wedding March* has begun.

Desperate to make an entrance and determined to not make her groom wait any longer, the bride asks, "Won't someone take me in? Can't you see it's time for me to go in?" But the ministers in the foyer brush off the request, saying, "No, you go on without us."

The bride decides to walk the aisle alone. Fearfully thinking all eyes will be on her and ashamed of her appearance, she enters the sanctuary. Only the groom notices her. His eyes are red and swollen from crying because He knows His bride had forgotten Him. He knows she was unprepared.

Much to the bride's surprise, standing in the midst of the altar, a prophet was speaking the Word of the Lord to the handful of guests that remained even though the ceremony is nearly an hour late. Unnoticed by the onlookers, the bride quickly takes her place next to the groom. She knows in her heart she has missed hearing the most important portion of the prophetic Word.

Motioning to a large banqueting table, the prophet continues to address the groom, saying: "I longed to fellowship with your entire family around this table, but because of distractions, only these few have come." With a sweeping motion, the prophet turns to address the bride and the rest of the congregation, saying, "And *all* these things have happened because of a lack of praying in other tongues."

Then the prophet turns and sits down. The bride, upset at missing the first part of the prophetic utterance, asks the prophet to repeat it. The reply is simple and direct: "The Word has been spoken. I cannot change or repeat it."

As we consider the meaning of this dream, there were several points the Spirit of God witnessed to my heart:

- The prevailing theme of the whole revelation is *distractions, distractions, distractions.*

- The mother, representing previous generations, was clearly more concerned with outward adornment, *forgetting entirely the importance of proper foundations.*

- The ministers in the lobby—symbolic of organized religion— are often *more concerned with the business of ministry rather than an understanding of the times.*

- *The simple solution to the fiasco is more praying in other tongues.* In order for the bride of Christ to be on time and properly adorned, believers must be given to prayer in the Spirit as never before.

For the past few years, I've had a specific burden to pray for the spiritual condition of the Church as a whole. I firmly believe that Spirit-filled Christians have a responsibility in prayer to help the entire body of Christ step in to a more mature understanding of spiritual things. Let us be ever vigilant and watchful as we see the day of Jesus' return approaching.

DOES ANYBODY KNOW WHAT TIME IT IS?

It Won't Be Long Now

*I*f there's one thing for sure in this day and age, it is that much of the Church, and definitely the world, have little or no idea just how late the hour has become toward Jesus' return. I don't profess to be a teacher of Bible prophecy, but the Lord wants some things brought to light about the hour in which we're living.

Many have said for decades, even centuries, that the coming of the Lord is near. Yet, so many have hardened their hearts to the timetable the Lord has laid out in His Word. When it comes to issues such as this, we should not base our beliefs on what someone else says. We should gain a thorough understanding of the Bible for ourselves and firmly establish the issue in our own hearts.

The apostle Peter encouraged believers this way: "Beloved, *be not ignorant of this one thing,* that *one day* is with the Lord as *a thousand years,* and *a thousand years as one day.* The Lord is not slack concerning his promise, as some men count slackness; but is longsuffering to usward, not willing that any should perish, but that all should come to repentance" (2 Peter 3:8-9).

God's time clock is much different than ours. Symbolically in the Scriptures, 2,000 years marks the passing of two days. Even if our calendars were off a by a few years as some theologians believe, we're now fully into the early hours of what the Lord would term "the third day."

There are many passages in the Bible that reference "the third day" whether actual events or prophetic revelation. Let's take a closer look at some of them to give us a better understanding of where we are now.

The first illustration that comes to mind is the resurrection of Jesus Christ. According to Matthew 16:21, Jesus made it clear to his disciples before His death that "...he must go to Jerusalem...and be killed, and be raised again *the third day.*" And, of course, He did just that (Matthew 27 and 28; Mark 16).

As a sidenote, it's important to realize that the Bible refers to believers as the body of Christ: "Now ye are the body of Christ, and members in particular" (1 Corinthians 12:27).

Also, Paul said in 1 Thessalonians 4:16-17, "For the Lord Himself will descend from heaven with a shout, with the voice of an archangel, and with the trumpet of God. And the dead in Christ will rise first. Then we who are alive *and* remain shall be caught up together with them in the clouds to meet the Lord in the air. And thus, we shall always be with the Lord."

We know from scripture that the Church—the body of Christ, the saints, the bride—will be caught up together with the Lord. Most believers fondly refer to this as the Rapture of the Church.

God is consistent. Throughout the Bible He gives little glimpses of His plans by using symbolic or prophetic events. Some Bible scholars believe if God raised up the first body of Christ (Jesus) early on the third day, then the catching away of the saints (the body of Christ) will happen "early on the third day."

We'll not examine the differences between the catching away of the saints (1 Thessalonians 4:16-17) and the Second Coming of Christ (His return to earth to rule and reign). However, most theologians agree there is only a matter of three and one-half to seven literal years separating the two events. In this chapter, we're specifically addressing the catching away of the saints.

A second passage of scripture that confirms this line of thinking can be found in the Old Testament. The prophet said in Hosea 6:1-2, "Come, and let us return unto the LORD...*After two days* He will revive us: on *the third day* He will raise us up, that we may live in His sight."

Another interesting passage related to this subject is somewhat of a surprise to me. Over the years, I've often wondered why God chose to have Jesus turn water into wine as His first miracle. As we examine this story in light of what we've been discussing, it becomes much clearer.

Look with me at John 2 where you'll notice the first words of the chapter are, "And *the third day....*" I believe without a shadow of doubt that this passage is symbolic and prophetic of the day and hour we're living in now.

There's a lot that can be gleaned from this narrative, but let's focus on just a few facets for the sake of time:

- Jesus' mother told the servants, "Whatsoever he saith unto you, do it" (verse 5 KJV). As servants of the Lord in this late hour, we must keep ourselves ready, willing, and able. When He speaks to our hearts, we should not step back or question. To borrow one of today's well-known advertising phrases: *Just do it!*

- The stone vessels filled with new wine were pots used in ceremonial cleansing (verse 6). It's vitally important we endeavor to keep ourselves pure and clean so we can be vessels fit for the Master's use.

- One benefit of our being pure vessels is that we, too, can be filled with new wine (verse 7). Let's stay filled to overflowing with the Spirit of God and power of God, drinking in and partaking of all the benefits of our covenant.

- Once the vessels were filled, the Lord was able to draw out of them what was needed (verse 8). God has made rich investments in His children. As we approach this late hour, it's important to make ourselves available to Him so He might draw upon the gifts He's placed in us to accomplish His purposes and plans.

- All who were present knew that the best wine had been saved for last (verse 10). God has saved His best for last! This was the beginning of miracles (verse 11). As we enter into *the third day,* we should expect to see miracles, signs, and wonders—miracles in our own lives, the lives of our family and friends, and in the lives of those yet to become children of God.

Finally, notice one more thing about this passage in verse 1 where it says, *"...the third day there was a marriage...."*

Revelation 19 tells of the marriage supper of the Lamb. Once the Lord—the Bridegroom—is reunited with His bride in glory, there will be a marriage celebration:

Revelation 19:5-9

Then a voice came from the throne, saying, "Praise our God, all you His servants and those who fear Him, both small and great!" And I heard, as it were, the voice of a great multitude, as the sound of many waters and as the sound of mighty thunderings, saying, "Alleluia! For the Lord God Omnipotent reigns! Let us be glad and rejoice and give Him glory, for the marriage of the Lamb has come, and His wife has made herself ready." And to her it was granted to be arrayed in fine linen, clean and bright, for the fine linen is the righteous acts of the saints.

Then he said to me, "Write: 'Blessed *are* those who are called to the marriage supper of the Lamb!' " And he said to me, "These are the true sayings of God."

It won't be long now! God's Word *will* come to pass. We must be watchful and make ourselves ready (Matthew 25:1-13).

AN UNUSUAL ASSIGNMENT

Humility is an Important Key to Success and Survival

I was called to the ministry at the age of 17 and sensed that God wanted me to be a preacher, but my denomination didn't believe in women in the pulpit. Every inquiry made indicated that I would have to settle for being a singer, a Sunday school teacher, or a missionary. Thinking that God was asking me to do something that was against the rules, I rebelled, which spiraled into 19 months of backsliding. When I came back to the Lord at the age of 21, it was through music that He wooed me—by His good grace and warm embrace.

After Bible school and several years thereafter, we were mostly involved in the ministry of helps. On April 19, 1994, the call and anointing of an evangelist was received—after more than 10 years of training, proving, and service. It was my first and true calling, as is evidenced by the emphasis upon the harvest in my teachings, the gifts of the Spirit, and the operation of gifts of healings and working of miracles. It still is the underlying motivator in just about everything we do. While we were still working in the ministry of helps in Oklahoma, we began to travel mostly on weekends as our work schedules permitted.

In 1997, the Lord released us from the ministry we were serving in Oklahoma. We moved to Branson, Missouri, and launched our own ministry. Bryan and I thought we would be traveling full time for the rest of our lives, but something didn't feel right. About three months after the move, I finally asked the Lord about it. His reply caught me off guard. I didn't speak a word of it to another living soul for at least three years—not even Bryan. The Lord said, "When you leave this place (Branson), you'll be pastoring."

"What?!" My points of contention were mostly based on this one thing: "I don't have the right personality to be a pastor." Yet my arguments were in vain. When I reluctantly broke the news to my husband around the year 2000, we made it a matter of dedicated prayer. In 2003, we moved back to Indiana to start a work.

Becoming an evangelist was like slipping on a lovely warm overcoat. It was easy for others to see; it was a good fit. Becoming a pastor, on the other hand, was like trying to put on a wetsuit—a struggle from the start. Once I wiggled into it, it fit like a glove, but oh, the struggle that ensued getting there.

The final six months of prayer before we moved from Branson produced a steady stream of "download," journaling page after page of vision and direction from the Father regarding the new assignment. At the time, I did not realize He was sending us to one of the poorest communities in the State of Indiana, which I like to refer to as the capital of small-town America.

The commission started something like this: "The first thing I want you to do is to develop a prayer group that will pray for economic development. What I want to do in the community is bigger than what the economy can support, and it's not just about one church."

It's true that God can build a mega-church in the middle of nowhere, but most often He chooses to work within the economy of a local community or region. So, the assignment was clear, and we did just what He told us to do.

For a little more than two years, a prayer group of predominantly new believers met in our home every Thursday at noon. We prayed faithfully for economic development for the community. The more we prayed for the community, the more community-minded we became. It wasn't long before we were taking on community-wide outreaches and events, developing ways to work with other churches as well as developing a few regional public feeding programs. Even though I'm not called to be an apostle, we know what it is to do an apostolic work. For example, Timothy, as a pastor, was called to do the work of an evangelist (2 Timothy 4:5). It's scriptural for five-fold ministry assignments to overlap and be layered upon one another to meet whatever purpose the Lord sees fit.

After two years, the anointing for the economic development prayer assignment lifted. I thought it odd but recognized we were about to transition. In fact, a wise woman of prayer once told me, "If you pray for the nations, you will go to the nations." Well, I didn't have a clue that the same principle would apply to prayer for "economic development," and I never could have guessed what was to come next.

Seemingly out of the blue, I received a call from the local economic development agency. They were looking for a part-time director and wondered if I would be interested in the job. I didn't even take time to pray about it. We had been praying about it for more than two years. I took the job: 15 hours per week with an annual budget for the entire organization of $22,000, including my salary. Remember that business degree the Lord wanted me to finish? Never underestimate the power of the Lord to utilize long-forgotten aspects of your resume.

I could write an entire book about *all* that the Lord did during the next eight years, but I will list here for you the sum of it. After five years, we had a staff of four working a total of 100 hours per week with an annual budget of $225,000. Membership in the organization grew by 87%. After six years, a $6 billion corporation contacted our office declaring their intention to move their base of operations to our community. This was a $30 million investment with an estimated economic impact of $260 million within the first 10 years of operation. All this, and pastoring full-time too, represented long hours, hard work, and a great deal of responsibility.

The real shocker for me was that the details for the *big* deal rested squarely on my shoulders. It was my responsibility to coordinate negotiations between the corporation, property owners, and local officials as well as balancing the demands of state and federal agencies. When the final contracts were officially signed, I walked out of the meeting and the Lord said, "You're done. You've accomplished what I sent you here to do. You can leave now." We stayed in the community for another 18 months, wrapping up things with the church, but our assignment was over.

Looking back, we were pioneers in the truest sense of the word. Sometimes God will give a believer an assignment that is "out of the box." The entire time we were pastoring, I could not find one colleague in ministerial circles who understood the work the Lord had given us to do. They would check on us and leave scratching their heads, saying, "You're doing what?" The whole economic development thing did not fit into their "box" of ministerial assignments. They could not relate to it and had no sincere appreciation for the work God was doing.

I won't take time to go into the details of it, but I will say economic development is a marathon not a sprint. I had a profound sense of destiny and recognized that the work we did would have a far-reaching impact into the future. The ground work had been laid for the sustainability of that community for generations. It's not for me to question why it was so important to the plan of God to move in such a profound way for such a small, insignificant place, but *move* He did. Who am I to question it?

When the assignment ended, little did we know we were about to embark upon the biggest transition of our lives. It was painful and hard. We had thrown our lives into the community, and we were disappointed when the Lord said we were done. We thought we would be there until Jesus' return. But the Lord had other assignments for us, and we have now embarked upon the adventure of a lifetime.

THE SUFFICIENCY
OF GRACE

God's Grace—An Essential Force for Believers Today

Hebrews 4:16

Let us therefore come boldly to the throne of grace, that we may obtain mercy and find grace to help in time of need.

*I*n the early days of our ministry, we worked full-time for one of the leading ministers in the land, as previously mentioned. This minister would receive on average 10,000 pieces of mail per week. Of course, there was no way for him personally to answer every single letter, but it was his expressed wish that every letter receives a reply. Most of the correspondence could be handled through a standardized processing system of readers and data entry operators. A department of approximately 40 people helped to process the huge volume of mail.

My job was to research and respond to the letters that could not be handled through normal channels. I had a library of letters this minister had written over the years on every subject one could possibly imagine. This was a necessary resource for handling the hard cases, the letters no one else could answer. So, for nearly eight years day in and day out, a steady of stream of hundreds of letters crossed my desk each week—terminal illness, doctrinal questions, the saddest stories, and the most difficult circumstances.

I did not realize at the time what a difficult position it was. Yet, looking back, I can see it could have taken its toll on me, were it not for the grace of God. I was a young wife and mother of two who worked a full-time job and daily faced mammoth problems that crossed my desk.

Each morning I would get in the shower and begin to go over the previous days' letters in my head—searching for direction and answers from the Father above. I would cry and plead to Him from the passage out of Hebrews 4:16, "God I need Your help. I am boldly approaching Your throne of grace for help in time of need. I can't get through this day without it. I've got to have Your grace." And it would come to me. Day after day, it was my routine, my plea. It was my victory.

The word *grace* is most commonly defined by theologians as *God's unmerited favor,* which is accurate and noteworthy. I've also heard it defined in the form of an acronym *G-R-A-C-E: God's Riches at Christ's Expense*—also noteworthy. Furthermore, Paul describes the grace of God in 2 Corinthians 9:8 as *being a super abundant supply.* It provides whatever is necessary in the circumstances of life.

After many years of practical application and petition, I've come to have an even deeper understanding of the word *grace.* Denise's paraphrased definition of *grace* goes something like this: *God's strength and His ability working in and through us to help us get through circumstances when we do not have any ability in and of ourselves.*

The apostle Paul is a man who had a need for grace. In fact, there is much controversy over Paul's thorn in the flesh in 2 Corinthians 12. Regardless of the nature of Paul's thorn, the conversation was simple. Paul said, "God, please make it stop!" God's reply was, *"My grace is sufficient for thee…"* (verse 9 KJV).

The problem arises with our Western way of thinking. If we were to ask most believers in America and even beyond what God meant when He said "My grace is sufficient," we would likely hear an answer that goes something like this, "Too bad, Paul. You're just going to have to put up with it." But that is not what God was saying—not at all.

Let's do a little word study. We've already defined *grace*, but let's also examine the Greek definition of the word *sufficient* to get a full understanding of the matter. In our society, *sufficient* implies *just enough*, but in the original Greek, it means so much more. According to Strong's Exhaustive Concordance, the word carries a strong connotation of *joy* and means *the idea of raising a barrier, to ward off, to avail.*

In other words, when God said to Paul, "My grace is sufficient for thee," He was saying, "Paul, My grace—My strength and My ability—working in and through you is enough to put a barrier around you, to ward off every attack of the enemy, and cause you to avail in every situation." Folks, that's something to shout about! Read it again. Wow!

Let's take it a step further. Earlier in this book, we briefly discussed the believer's position of being seated in heavenly places in Christ (Ephesians 2:6), far above all principality, and power, and might and dominion, and every name that is named (Ephesians 1:21). This passage references the same throne mentioned in Hebrews 4:16 because the throne of God is the throne of grace. If we're seated together with Christ, we're actually seated together with Him on that throne of *grace!* Finding grace to help in time of need shouldn't be an issue if we're taking our place in Him. His grace is more than sufficient for the day and hour in which we live.

As we go forward in these last days, we need to rely on the grace of God like never before. His strength is made perfect in our weakness. We have no power in ourselves to accomplish the work set before us but with God's grace all things are possible!

FULL CIRCLE

Look What the Lord Has Done!

*D*uring the time we lived in Branson, Missouri, we were numbered among the first corporate group at Prayer Mountain in the Ozarks. In fact, we left Oklahoma in response to a call from the Lord to learn from Dr. Billye Brim. She is a well-seasoned minister of the gospel and a woman of prominence in the Spirit. I thank God for her wisdom and dedication to the things of God.

Even though we were reluctant to leave our positions in Oklahoma, the Lord assured us that the move was the next phase of ministry and education for us. The time spent with her and the people of prayer in Missouri has proven over and over to be one of the wisest investments we could ever have made.

During the years at Prayer Mountain, Sister Billye paraded countless numbers of seasoned men and women of prayer into the corporate prayer sessions with us. These men and women were well schooled in old-time Pentecostal methods of prayer. Many of them have now moved on into their heavenly rewards.

One of our beloved leaders, Martha Eufaula McGee (a niece to the great Blackwood Brothers quartet of years gone by) was a sergeant in the prayer room. I think of her most often these days as I find myself doing things that I learned from her—prayer secrets that could only be "caught." Brother Hagin used to say, "Prayer is best caught, not taught." It was at Prayer Mountain that we came to fully understand this concept and learned by doing.

Many of the members of our "class" have moved on to hold important positions in the realm of the spirit. One of the ladies with whom we prayed should be respected as one of the leading intercessors in the world. She and her husband went on to live in Moscow for many years, working closely with one of the most significant ministers of our time. She's a bull in the prayer closet. It takes great faith and tenacity to be able to handle a long-term prayer assignment such as Moscow, Russia. The powers of darkness know best not to mess with her. I'm honored to call her my friend and remember fondly the years we spent together in Branson, learning from the best of the best in prayer.

Fast forward to 2014 when the sabbatical we took after pastoring in Indiana was a return to Branson. I needed to find center again if I was going to step into this new five-fold ministry office with excellence. Speaking candidly, the pressures of pastoring and economic development had sucked the life out of my prayer life. It was to a point where I had stopped singing, which is a bad sign. It was in the prayer sessions with Billye and her family and all the wonderful people at Prayer Mountain that I found my voice again. When it returned, it came with such a powerful unction, it sometimes was difficult to contain.

Six months into our sabbatical, we received the commission to go into "the many nations of the earth," but as we approached the 12-month mark, we had no further direction. I know the Lord was taking time to let us transition to the new office and to heal, but we were anxious to know what came next. One day in June of 2015, as I pressed the Lord for answers, He suddenly declared, "I want you back in Terre Haute by August 1."

"What?" was the question that rose up in our hearts—a question I seem to ask the Lord a lot. "What does returning to Terre Haute, Indiana, have to do with going to the nations?" It should be noted I had this same conversation with the Lord in 1987 upon graduation from Bible school (page 70). Meanwhile, here's a preview. The answer from the Lord has proven to be: "Everything!"

Terre Haute, Indiana, is my husband's home town. It's the city where I attended college. It is the city where we met and spent the first year of our marriage together, but it no longer was a place we considered home after being gone for more than 26 years.

Yet, we've been walking by faith long enough to not even question. With the blessing of our pastor and friends in Branson, we packed up and moved with no additional direction. Not that we didn't seek it, because we did. We prayed fervently, but received nothing until the moving van was loaded, and we were literally driving cross-country. With my hands on the steering wheel, the Lord began to cast vision: "I want you to start a prayer school for the nations. I want you to take a cross-section of pray-ers from all the Spirit-filled churches of the city and teach them how to pray together corporately."

My faith-filled reply was, "That will never work, God." Yet, within 10 days of our arrival in Terre Haute, God had strategically connected us with a group of pastors who had been praying together for more than seven years. Thursday mornings became the highlight of our week. These times of prayer were not about the individual churches, but about the city—their city. It was not unusual to see these men of God heaped together in the floor pouring their hearts out for the souls of their city. No wonder the city is in revival! Not only that, but most of them had visions to go to the nations. They would support each other in multiple ways, like attending one another's special services, going on missions trips together, etc.

It was in these prayer sessions that I began to see that God's idea for a citywide prayer school might work. If the pastors were willing to pray together in unity, perhaps the people of their churches would, too. So, we did it. We launched a Saturday morning prayer school for the nations the next spring. For nine months, we ran a weekly circuit between five different churches. The pray-ers showed up to pray—not just at their own churches but to all the other churches, too. And we prayed. We learned to pray together as one, and we touched the nations. Attendees began to fondly refer to the sessions as *adventures in prayer*. One young woman said, "I love this school. We get to *go* places."

As our ministry travel schedule increased, eventually we were able to transition the school into the hands of the pastors and key leaders who were participating each week. The students became the teachers and shared the principles they learned within their own congregations. Each pastor who opened their doors to the school will testify to the fact that it dramatically impacted the atmosphere of their churches and the city. The heavens were opened in such a way it had not been seen before.

We have now taken the "show on the road," so-to-speak. The same principles we taught in Terre Haute, we teach in other communities and regions in the United States and in the nations. Our local pastor is an apostle in the truest definition of the office. Sometimes we get to work together with him by doing advanced prayer work before he goes into a city or a nation. We don't just pray, but we work with local churches and pastors, developing a sense of unity and purpose in their prayer ministries prior to the arrival of the apostolic teams that bring outpouring and revival.

Since returning to Terre Haute in 2015, we've seen consistent outpourings of the Spirit there as well as great unity and love among pastors. The Lord has added this instruction to our call to the nations: "Yes, I am sending you to the many nations of the earth. And every-where you go, you will tell of what you have seen and heard here in Terre Haute, Indiana."

Ephesians 4:1-6

I, therefore, the prisoner of the Lord, beseech you to walk worthy of the calling with which you were called, with all lowliness and gentleness, with longsuffering, bearing with one another in love, endeavoring to keep the unity of the Spirit in the bond of peace. There is one body and one Spirit, just as you were called in one hope of your calling; one Lord, one faith, one baptism; one God and Father of all, who is above all, and through all, and in you all.

Ephesians 4:11-13

And He Himself gave some to be apostles, some prophets, some evangelists, and some pastors and teachers, for the equipping of the saints for the work of ministry, for the edifying of the body of Christ, till we all come to the unity of the faith and of the knowledge of the Son of God, to a perfect man, to the measure of the stature of the fullness of Christ.

Bryan and I have a strong sense now of having come full circle. We work with a lot of people with ties to our past, present, and future. When we lived in Terre Haute before, we longed to see the things we are now witnessing in the city. It has been a super-great blessing to catch a glimpse of the work that God has done and continues to do in the hearts and lives of the people in Terre Haute.

When we lived in Terre Haute in the first year of our marriage, we did not have any understanding of being linked to any sort of long-term assignment or work there. But now we certainly have a sense of fulfillment and a sort of completion of a divinely ordered call that He began in our hearts so many years ago. Over the horizon, the nations loom in our hearts, but for now, we celebrate Terre Haute, Indiana. Look what the Lord has done!

THE BRIGHTNESS
OF HIS APPEARING

The Church Is Supposed to be Different

On Friday, March 16, 2007, I had made a long drive to Gatlinburg, Tennessee, to attend a women's conference. The guest speaker was my favorite mentor, and it was time for some refreshing. As a pastor, I didn't get out of town very often, so it was a treat to have a few days away from home. Plus, the date was special to me. Twenty-three years earlier on Friday, March 16, 1984, I had a profound visitation from the Lord—an experience that changed my life forever (page 22).

So, my expectations were high as I entered the meeting room that evening even though the only person that I recognized was the guest speaker. The conference host was a female pastor whom I had never met. The worship was outstanding, and the tangible presence of God filled the room. Even though my expectations were high, I never imagined what would happen next.

As the worship was wrapping to a close, in the front of the room directly before me, there stood a tall figure. His appearance was so startlingly bright I could hardly look upon it. Blinking through a glory-filled haze, I instinctively said, "Lord, what is that?"

Immediately, speaking in a firm, clear voice, He replied, "I am giving you a new vision of Myself to carry with you from now until My return. But it is not just a vision of Me but a picture of My body, the

Glorious Church, and what She will look like when I return for Her."
Stunned, I hardly knew what to do next.

Through tear-filled eyes, I watched as the conference host
approached the podium. Quietly, with an obvious tone of reverence,
she asked us to turn in our Bibles to a certain passage of scripture.
Before I mention the specific passage, I will remind you that I did not
know this woman, and I certainly had not had an opportunity to tell
her what I had just seen and heard. As far as I know, the experience was
mine alone.

I will also say that I have always had an affinity for the Word of
God, no matter what the Lord has allowed me to experience in the
realm of the Spirit. If I cannot find scriptural basis for it, I set it aside
until He chooses to back it up with the Word. On this occasion, before
I could even ask for this type of validation, He directed our hostess to
the podium.

She said slowly, "Turn with me in your Bibles to Matthew 17."
There are no words to describe what went on inside of me as I heard
her read: "After six days Jesus took with him Peter, James and John the
brother of James, and led them up a high mountain by themselves.
There He was transfigured before them. *His face shone like the sun and
His clothes became as white as the light."* That was it! She read the exact
description of what I had just seen standing before me, clearly written
in the Word of God.

I don't remember anything else the conference host said that night.
For the rest of the meetings, the guest speaker delivered powerful messages on the believer's authority. I went home refreshed and moved
beyond words at the gloriousness of His appearing. Again, I was forever
changed.

Upon my return, I told a few members of my congregation about it, but for the most part over the years, I've guarded that moment in my heart. Yet, I also have somehow known that God would eventually require me to tell it. I believe that time is now.

Has the transfiguration of Christ been a mystery to you? I've always loved the story (Matthew 17:1-8; Mark 9:2-8). Yet, until that night, I never understood what God was really trying to show the disciples. Certainly, there is more to the story than just the brightness of His appearing.

For now, let's focus on the revelation at hand. We have come to such a time as this. It is time for the glorious Church (Ephesians 5:27) to put on Her robe of righteousness and walk in all of Her God-given authority. Jesus is not the only One who will be glorious at His appearing. "Arise, shine, for your light has come! The glory of the Lord is risen upon you!" (Isaiah 60:1).

The Church is Supposed to be Different.

And now is the time for the Church to shine!

NO JESUS, NO PEACE

Know Jesus, Know Peace

The word *peace* in the original Hebrew is *Shalom*. Simply defined *shalom* means *the peace that comes from being whole—whole* meaning *nothing missing, nothing broken*. It is not possible to know true peace without knowing the Prince of Peace, Jesus Christ. When we enter a relationship with the Lord, we find what it truly means to know peace.

Often Christianity is confused with other religions of the world. Yet in reality, Christianity is not about *religion*—it's about *relationship*. A relationship with the Lord Jesus Christ brings peace that passes all understanding.

Perhaps you have never known the peace that comes from being whole; the peace that comes from knowing Him. Then this section is designed for you! Perhaps some readers already know Him as Lord but have strayed in their relationship with Him. Let's not drift so far from Him that we cease to intimately experience His wonderful ways.

It's not difficult to enter a relationship with the Savior. Romans 10:9-10 says, "That if thou shalt confess with thy mouth the Lord Jesus, and shalt believe in thine heart that God hath raised him from the dead, thou shalt be saved. For with the heart man believeth unto righteousness; and with the mouth confession is made unto salvation." It's that simple.

I encourage you to pray this prayer aloud now:

Dear heavenly Father, I come to you in the name of Jesus. I believe He is your Son. He died on the cross for my sins, and You raised Him from the dead. He is now seated at Your right hand. Because I believe, I confess Jesus as my Lord and Savior. I receive Him as my Lord and receive forgiveness for all my sins. According to Your Word, as I believe and confess, I am saved. Thank You, Lord, for saving me and cleansing me with the precious blood of Jesus. Thank You, Lord, for loving me unconditionally. I receive Your love and purpose in my heart to live for You. In Jesus' name. Amen.

If you have prayed this prayer, welcome to the family of God! Share your good news with us at www.adorationinternational.org/contact and let us know what God has done in your life.

ABOUT THE AUTHOR

 Bryan and Denise Shaw are full-time traveling ministers, missionaries, and corporate prayer specialists. They established Adoration Ministries, Inc. in 1998. The Shaws traveled extensively throughout North America until 2003 when they founded and pastored a small church in south-central Indiana for 11 years. In 2016, the Shaws established a citywide prayer school for the nations in Terre Haute, Indiana. In 2019, they launched a series of prayer seminars featuring world-class guest speakers.

Bryan is a graduate of Life Christian Center's Bible School in Branson, Missouri, and Denise is a graduate of RHEMA Bible Training Center in Broken Arrow, Oklahoma.

The couple has been married for more than 30 years and currently make their home in Indiana. They have two beautiful daughters, a treasured son-in-law, and two precious grandchildren.